SELF-MANAGEMENT

STUDIES IN COMPARATIVE POLITICS
Peter H. Merkl, Series Editor

Rights and Liberties in the World Today:
Constitutional Promise & Reality

Ivo D. Duchacek
•
Power Maps:
Comparative Politics of Constitutions

Ivo D. Duchacek
•
German Foreign Policies, West & East:
On the Threshold of a New European Era

Peter H. Merkl
•
Political Culture & Group Conflict
in Communist China

Alan P. L. Liu
•
Nazi Youth in the Weimar Republic

Peter Stachura
•
Women in the World:
A Comparative Study

Lynn Iglitzin, Ruth Ross
•
Self-Management:
New Dimensions to Democracy

Ichak Adizes, Elisabeth Mann Borgese
•
The Comparative Policy Process

T. Alexander Smith

SELF-MANAGEMENT:
New Dimensions to Democracy

EDITED BY

Ichak Adizes

Elisabeth Mann Borgese

*This book has been published
with the encouragement and support of
the Center for the Study of Democratic Institutions,
Santa Barbara, California*

SANTA BARBARA, CALIFORNIA
OXFORD, ENGLAND

492497

© 1975 by The Fund for the Republic, Inc.

Library of Congress Cataloging in Publication Data

Main entry under title:

Self-management.

    (Studies in comparative politics ; 7)
    Partial proceedings of a conference held at the Center for the Study of Democratic Institutions, Oct. 1971; with additional papers.
    1. Employees' representation in management—Congresses. I. Adizes, Ichak, ed. II. Borgese, Elisabeth Mann, ed. III. Center for the Study of Democratic Institutions. IV. Series.
HD5650.S43   658.31'52   74-34220
ISBN 0-87436-202-4
ISBN 0-87436-203-2 pbk.

American Bibliographical Center—Clio Press, Inc.
2040 Alameda Padre Serra
Santa Barbara, California

European Bibliographical Center—Clio Press
Woodside House, Hinksey Hill
Oxford OX1 5BE, England

Designed by Jack Swartz
Composed by Camera-Ready Composition
Printed and bound in the United States of America.

To the People of Yugoslavia

CONTENTS

vii

BIOGRAPHICAL NOTES

Ichak Adizes: Associate Professor of Managerial Studies at the Graduate School of Management and Associate Research Fellow, Institute of Industrial Relations, U.C.L.A., and a Visiting Fellow at the Center for the Study of Democratic Institutions, Santa Barbara, 1972. Dr. Adizes has done extensive research on Yugoslavia, and has lectured in Yugoslavia, Israel, Peru, Chile, Brazil, Mexico and Sweden to various programs. Among his publications: *Industrial Democracy—Yugoslav Style* (New York: Free Press, 1971).

Arthur G. Anderson: IBM Vice-President, and President, General Products Division. Dr. Anderson received his bachelor's degree in physics from the University of San Francisco and a Ph.D. degree in physics from New York University in 1958. He is a Fellow of the American Physical Society, a member of the American Association for the Advancement of Science, the New York Academy of Science, and a senior member of the Institute of Electrical and Electronic Engineers. In August 1970 he became a Visiting Fellow at the Center for the Study of Democratic Institutions; he rejoined IBM in June 1971.

Harry S. Ashmore: President of the Center for the Study of Democratic Institutions at Santa Barbara. In 1957 he was awarded the Pulitzer Prize in history for distinguished service in the Little Rock school integration controversy. From 1960 to 1963 Mr. Ashmore served as editor-in-chief of *Encyclopaedia Britannica,* and as director of editorial research and development from 1963 to 1967. He has been a correspondent for the *New York Herald Tribune,* has written articles for many leading magazines, and is the author of five books: *The Negro and the Schools, An Epitaph for Dixie, The Other Side of Jordan, The Man in the Middle,* and *Mission to Hanoi* (with William C. Baggs).

Elisabeth Mann Borgese: Senior Fellow of the Center for the Study of Democratic Institutions, and the daughter of Thomas Mann. Mrs. Borgese is the author of *Ascent of Woman, To Whom It May Concern, The Language Barrier, Only the Pyre* (a play), and

The Ocean Regime. She has written a number of stories and essays for American and Italian magazines and anthologies. She has also done many translations of books on art and musicology. Currently she is working on a book entitled *The World Communities.*

Silviu Brucan: Professor of International Relations, University of Bucharest, and author of *The Dissolution of Power* (New York: Knopf, 1971). Dr. Brucan was Rumania's Ambassador to the United Nations and is presently an Associate Fellow of the Center for the Study of Democratic Institutions.

Manuel Echeverria: President of the Workers Council of Cooperativa SODIMAC, Santiago de Chile, Chile.

Fred E. Emery: Senior research fellow at the Research School of Social Science in the Australian National University, Canberra. After graduating from the University of Melbourne, he spent his first years as an applied social scientist on problems of communication and social change. During the 1960s he was a senior member of the Human Resources Program at the Tavistock Institute of Human Relations in London. He has played a leading role in developing and applying systems approach to organizational change in Britain, Norway, and, at present, Australia.

Edward Kardelj: Member, Council of Federation, Presidency of the League of Communists of Yugoslavia, Dr. h.c. University of Ljubljana. He is a member of several Academies, and has published several treatises and books concerning social sciences: "Socialism and War," "Socialist Policy in the Countryside," "The Problems of Our Socialist Development" (8 vols.).

Pressley McCoy: For nine years associate director of the Danforth Foundation, followed by three years as the first president of the Central States College Association. In 1968 he became the first chancellor of Johnston College, which launched the nation's first self-management-in-learning program through the contract-evaluation system. Currently he is director of the Middle and University Colleges at United States International University.

William McWhinney: A co-creator of Open Systems Planning, an eclectic mode of creating psychic space for social and organizational engagement. He has been on the Faculty of Management at U.C.L.A. since 1963, after being at Leeds University in England and Carnegie-Mellon University.

Fred Warner Neal: Chairman of the International Relations Faculty at Claremont Graduate School. Dr. Neal has written extensively on Yugoslav affairs, including *Titoism in Action* (1958) and *Yugoslavia and the New Communism* (1962). An Associate of the Center for the Study of Democratic Institutions, he was earlier representative in

Yugoslavia for the American Universities Field Staff and Chief of Research on Eastern Europe in the State Department.

Joze Pacek: Secretary-Treasurer, Slovenian Parliament, Yugoslavia.

Arvid Pardo: Educated in Italy, France, England, and Switzerland, he served as United Nations official from 1945 to 1964. From 1964 until 1971 he served as the Ambassador of Malta to the United Nations, and since 1971 he has been the Ambassador of Malta for Ocean Affairs and a Fellow of the Woodrow Wilson International Center for Scholars. In 1971 he was a Visiting Fellow of the Center for the Study of Democratic Institutions.

Najdan Pasic: Dean, Faculty of Political Science, Belgrade University, and Chairman of the Serbian Delegation to the Federal Parliament.

William Pennell Rock: Former research assistant at the Center for the Study of Democratic Institutions, he did graduate work at Kings College, Cambridge. He spent two years as a senior research fellow at the Center for Advanced Study in Philosophy at Benares Hindu University, and studied for a year at the C.G. Jung Institute in Switzerland.

Einar Thorsrud: Senior research fellow at the Work Research Institute in Oslo. Graduating from the University of Oslo, he worked first as research fellow, then as an applied social scientist in industry until he became director of the Institute for Industrial Social Research at the Technical University in Trondheim, Norway. During the 1960s he was director of the Industrial Democracy Program in Norway, which consisted of a large number of field experiments and programs for organizational change under the sponsorship of trade unions and employers' organizations. At present he is director of a research program for organizational change in Norwegian shipping.

Anton Vratusa: Yugoslavian diplomat and formerly a professor at the School of Political Sciences in Belgrade. Since 1967 he has been a member of the Permanent Mission of Yugoslavia to the United Nations.

Harvey Wheeler: Senior Fellow of the Center for the Study of Democratic Institutions. Dr. Wheeler received his A.B. and M.A. degrees from Indiana University, and his Ph.D. from Harvard. He taught political science at Harvard and at Johns Hopkins University. Mr. Wheeler is the coauthor, with the late Eugene Burdick, of the novel *Fail-Safe,* and is the author of *The Politics of Revolution* and editor of *Beyond the Punitive Society.*

Yehuda Yudin: Chairman of the Department of Workers' Participation in Management of the Histadrut (General Federation of Labour in Israel); member of the Histadrut Executive Bureau and of the Executive Committee of "Hevrat Ovdim," the roof organization of

Labour Economy in Israel. He is editor of "Dapei Shituf," a journal devoted to problems of labor economy and industrial democracy; his is active in Trade Union Movement and international activities of the Histadrut. He is author of numerous articles in Israeli labor dailies and lecturer at the Workers' College in Tel-Aviv.

PREFACE

THE various articles assembled in this book were generated by social scientists and labor activists. Their main focus is upon workers' participation in decision-making as a means to democratize society or as a means to preserve its democratic character.

The book evolved out of a week-long discussion held in October 1971 at the Center for the Study of Democratic Institutions in Santa Barbara, California. Contained herein is an edited version of that discussion, some of the original papers prepared for that conference, and additional papers written specifically for this book to answer some of the questions which remained after the conference ended.

The significance of composing a book like this one is manifold. We brought together politicians, labor activists, and social scientists to enable us to obtain different views of the problems, the aspirations, and the experiences with democratic participative systems, and to give us cross-national comparisons.

We have purposely avoided heavily editing this material and have allowed material that is not absolutely supported by empirical evidence, because we want the reader to see for himself what the various motivations for encouraging participation were and then to judge for himself whether the experiences described met those expectations.

Furthermore, we purposely sought to raise as many aspects and questions regarding self-management as was possible, rather than seeking answers to any one of them. The extant literature on the topic of self-management is highly specialized and attempts to give answers to relatively well-bounded and limited problems. This book, by contrast, may appear inconclusive, touching on too many grounds at once without dealing in depth with any one in particular. This is simply a reflection of the complexity and comprehensiveness of the concept of self-management. It is the goal of the editors to expose readers to the many aspirations and the multiplicity of barriers in this field.

It might be helpful if the reader has done some prior reading on the Yugoslav experience with self-management to be able to fully comprehend the problems raised in this book; however, other readers as well will find the material of interest. This book raises disturbing questions, to which the reader himself will have to provide answers, for there are no set answers in this field.

In choosing material for this book, we focused upon the experiences of three different countries: Yugoslavia, Israel, and Norway. Four articles are devoted to the Yugoslav experience, and two articles to the others. We found this unequal distribution desirable for a specific reason. Yugoslavia has gone furthest towards developing a fully participative system for all of its organizations. The problems the Yugoslavs are facing in trying to advance economically without eroding the system have great significance for both totalitarian countries contemplating decentralization and for pluralistic systems seeking methods for retarding the strong drift towards centralization which poses a constant threat to democracy. An additional reason for heavy emphasis on Yugoslavia is the availability of papers from leading Yugoslav theoreticians concerning the latest thought about analysis of specific barriers to self-management prevailing in Yugoslavia.

Edward Kardelj discusses one of the most significant and most troublesome concepts of the Yugoslav self-managed system: social ownership. According to this unique Yugoslav concept, society in general (not government) owns the accumulated assets of all organizations. The members of the organization do not own the assets and thus they cannot decrease the value of the company, i.e., sell off the assets to increase their income. They own only the results of their work, and they can only share in the income that they have generated themselves with these assets. The social capital or the accumulated assets belong to the society in general, which means to all and to no one.

This approach to capital has created several problems, including the concentration of capital in certain industries, the lack of sufficient capital mobility, and the emergence of relatively free, politically independent power centers such as banks and large companies which possess resources that others need to borrow. Kardelj recognizes the existence of capital; it is not its existence nor the fact that it shares in the distribution of income to which he objects, but rather the lack of societal control over this source of power. Capital, i.e., accumulated past labor, should be controlled by the people who accumulated those assets with their labor in the first place. He claims that to enable the creators of capital to control and benefit from it, government must not control it. This is one of the Yugoslav system's main points of departure from the statist economies.

In the quest for democracy, Kardelj clearly warns against the dependency of management on political affiliation which occurs when capital is dominated and concentrated in the hands of government, as in the U.S.S.R. For democracy to take place, Kardelj claims that management should be responsible to and dependent upon the people it manages.

Furthermore, Kardelj clearly states that a return to statist centralism is one of the alternatives that will have to be considered if the self-management system cannot overcome the difficulties it is presently experiencing in dealing with the problems of capital and its noncontrollable power.

The reader may become confused by the multitude of terms used by the various Yugoslav writers: past labor, living labor, necessary labor, surplus labor, etc. The point that should not be missed, however, is that the self-management system is seeking a new solution to an old problem: how to ensure that democracy will prevail in society, and that accumulated assets will not over time constitute a source of power that will endanger democracy and alienate the people by subordinating them to the production process.

Anton Vratusa raises other important issues. What is the role of the Communist Party in economic decentralization, and what was the reaction of the Party to the fact that the Party was required to remove its influence from economic activities and to disassociate itself from the managerial group? What are the limits to political decentralization? Vratusa claims that the Party was both the initiator of and the affected entity from this process of economic democratization. A process of depoliticization of political parties, which Vratusa claims has been a goal and a process in Yugoslavia, is a rare phenomenon which should attract the attention of social scientists while this process is taking place.

Vratusa also emphasizes another issue that Kardelj raises. How can self-management maintain itself while under pressure from two different sides? On the one hand, there is the danger from the government state bureaucracy (from which it seems to have escaped), and on the other hand, there is the danger from the increasing strength of a (relatively) socially uncontrolled technostructure which has more power than a democratic system ought to allow. The closer towards a market economy that Yugoslavia moves, the stronger become the powers of the technostructure or professional management. The more the government is called upon to remedy this, the greater the danger from a powerful government, again negating the principles of self-management.

In its struggle to preserve democracy, Yugoslavia is attempting to deprofessionalize political office. It is trying to avoid the pitfalls of a representative democracy, where the political interplay between professional politicians undermines the goals of direct involvement, direct democracy, and control of their own destiny by the people themselves.

Vratusa calls for a democracy based not on political parties, but on direct participation. "The traditional political party system is the basis of a representative parliamentary system in which the citizen is represented by a general representative elected for a given term. It necessarily becomes an instrument in the struggle for power and a source of political demagoguery no matter whether it is based on one or a number of political parties."

Mr. Pasic explores the essence of and the historical theoretical development of self-management, emphasizing the necessity for self-management of a market mechanism in the economic sphere, while Mr. Pacek deals with the fears that people had about self-management and the experiences of the system. These four articles complete the section on Yugoslavia.

A unique attribute of the Israeli situation is that it offers the whole spectrum of known systems of participation, coexisting side by side: the self-managed community (the kibbutz), cooperatives (moshavei ovdim), labor-managed enterprises with compulsory joint consultation, and private industry with participation afforded as the managers desire.

The Israeli case presented by Y. Yudin is of particular interest since it presents the role of participative systems in a society experiencing great turbulence from vast, rapid and extremely heterogeneous immigration, as well as analyzing the efforts to preserve self-management under these trying conditions. Was participation helpful in this adjustment to rapid immigration? How do people with different values accept participation? What difficulties did the system encounter due to differences in value systems?

Emery and Thorsrud introduce us to an alternative sociotechnical route taken by the Norwegians in their attempts to develop democracy in the working place, including the placing of worker representation on boards of directors. The Norwegian experience is of special interest since it represents a sociological-evolutionary approach to the problem of worker participation, and thus is different from the revolutionary, comprehensive approach of the Yugoslavs.

The edited discussion that took place at the Center in Santa Barbara (presented at the end of the book) focuses on several questions, including the following. Is social ownership an absolute necessity for democracy? Are competition and market mechanisms compatible with worker participation in decision-making and with self-management? Questions are asked about the role of political parties in a system that calls for maximum direct participation and depoliticization of the processes that lead to national decision-making.

The editors of this book have contributed to this volume in different ways. Elisabeth Mann Borgese explores the goals, aspirations, and promise of self-management to different countries at different points in their economic, political, and social development. Ichak Adizes defines the terms of self-management and participation, and discusses how the various systems around the world differ from each other in implementing participation. One of the topics on which Adizes focuses is the role and behavior of professional management, which, theoretically at least, should wither away in self-management, but which in reality turns out to be a very powerful force. It is frequently considered to be the main barrier to the implementation of industrial democracy.

In putting this book together, we have used some materials which were prepared for the conference and have since been published in professional publications. The portion of Ichak Adizes's contribution which deals with the role of management in democratic organizations has been published in a larger and more extended form under the title of "The Role of Management in Democratic (Communal) Organizational Structures," in *The Annals of Public and Co-Operative Economy,* October-December 1971, vol. 42, no. 4; the German version appeared in *Annalen Der Gemeinwirtschaf,* January-March 1972, vol. 41, no. 1; and the French version was published in *Les Annales de L'Economie Collective,* January-March 1973 vol. 61, no. 1. In Spanish, it appeared in *Gerencia* (Lima, Peru: IPAE) in two installments: Nov.-Dec. 1973 and Jan.-Feb. 1974 under the title "Gerencia y Estructuras Comunales." The Yugoslav translation appeared in *Moderna Organizacija* No. 6, 1972.

Elisabeth Mann Borgese's contribution previously appeared in *The Center Magazine,* May-June 1972, vol. 5, no. 3.

Kardelj's text is an adapted excerpt from *Contradictions of Social Property in Contemporary Socialist Practice* (Belgrade: Radnicka Stampa, 1972).

Thorsrud and Emery's article is an edited version of the same article published in the *Journal of Industrial Relations,* vol. 9, No. 2, February 1970.

Mr. Yudin's contribution in this book is a shortened version of a paper he submitted to the International Conference on the Role of Cooperative and Public Economies in Democratic Societies which was held in Tel Aviv, on May 22-25, 1973.

Every book has its "mother hen." We most gratefully acknowledge the work of our research assistant, Ms. Linda Battin. The endless hours she put in "babying" this book to its final draft, doing it with motivation and dedication, made this book's publication possible.

The book is partially supported by the Institute of Industrial Relations, U.C.L.A., and a grant from the Manpower Administration, U.S. Department of Labor, however it should be noted that points of view expressed in this book do not necessarily represent the policies of the Department of Labor of the Institute of Industrial Relations.

Grateful acknowledgment is also made to The Center for the Study of Democratic Institutions, which provided moral and financial support for this venture.

In light of the global movement to increase participation of people in the decisions that affect their lives, the topics discussed in this book are, we believe, of significance and worthy of attention.

Ichak Adizes

INTRODUCTION
The Promise of Self-management

by Elisabeth Mann Borgese

Senior Fellow, Center for the Study of Democratic Institutions
Santa Barbara, California

THE theory and practice of self-management will likely catch the imagination and mobilize the activities of people all over the world during the last quarter of this century.

What is self-management? What are the trends in contemporary history which may bring it into being, East, West, North, and South? And what are its chances of success in the post industrial society of the twenty-first century?

Self-management is the kernel of Yugoslav political theory and constitutional law as it has been developing since the 1950s. The Yugoslavs must have written hundreds of thousands of pages on the subject. They have enacted self-management in their economic, social, cultural, and political organizations. They have built it into their constitution. They are enforcing it in their courts and tribunals. And they are experimenting with it, elaborating, adapting, developing, enlarging it, and amending their constitution accordingly.

Self-management politicizes the economic enterprise by transforming it into a community which is not bent on profit-making exclusively but on articulating the social and political as well as the economic decision-making processes of its members, workers, and managers alike.

Every enterprise has its workers' council, elected by the total membership of the enterprise, on a one-man, one-vote basis. To prevent the professionalization of the workers' councils, members are elected for a period not exceeding two years, and no one can be reelected for a second consecutive term.

The workers' council is an autonomous body that makes its own internal rules and decisions with regard to policies and plans, the sharing of revenues, the allocation of resources, and any other business, even including security (each enterprise has its own self-managed contingent of the Peoples army).

Every enterprise also has its own executive committee whose members are elected from among the enterprise personnel. The executive committee is also headed by a director who is the chief manager of the enterprise. He is elected either by the workers' council or by the total membership and is responsible to the workers' council and the membership. He may provisionally suspend decisions of the workers council if he finds them in conflict with the law. A municipal court of arbitration will then make the final decision on the case.

Self-management, at the same time, depoliticizes the state by transforming it into a community which articulates not only the political, but the economic, social, and cultural decision-making processes of its members. This happens through a multichamber assembly system. At the federal, republican, and municipal levels, the representatives of the political community share their decision-making power with representatives of economic enterprises, scientific institutions, and public health institutions.

The micro-community of the enterprise and the macro-community of what used to be the state thus look very much alike. Both are multidimensional or polyvalent (that is, embracing all dimensions of human activity), and both are organized from the bottom up, not from the top down. Both are interacting, and it is through this interaction and by participating in decision-making at the governmental level that the self-managing community really creates and asserts its autonomy.

This kind of order may sound utopian, impractical at the level of economic efficiency, too complex, and much too idealistic. But the facts do not bear out such a view. For while the Yugoslavs have undoubtedly run into all sorts of difficulties in the elaboration and enactment of their far-from-perfect system, twenty years of self-management have had the following results. Per capita income has risen from two hundred dollars in 1950 to seven hundred dollars in 1970. Industrial output has increased fivefold (a portion of the additional G.N.P. is invested in industrial development and for communal purposes); the non-agricultural sector of the economy, embracing only thirty percent of the working population in 1950, has grown to fifty-three percent. Exports of goods and services have risen from twelve percent of the gross national product in 1950 to twenty percent in 1969, with over fifty percent of these exports consisting of manufactured goods. The real standard of living of the population has risen three hundred percent during the last twelve years.

Self-management in Yugoslavia has deep autochthonous roots in the communal systems of Slavic society. It has intellectual roots in Marxist theory—or that part of it that the Yugoslav leaders could use to graft on the indigenous growth (there is a mixture of autochthonous and universal, existential and intellectual factors in every revolution). And it has vigorous roots in the partisan movement that routed the fascist invaders in World War II and brought the new society into being.

There were hundreds of thousands of these partisans in the war. Bereft of means of communication, they received no orders. Lacking supplies of food, clothing, and arms, they had to rely on their own initiative and inventiveness and on the population around them. The partisan knew no distinction between soldier and civilian. He knew only people.

Partisan strategy, the Yugoslavs learned from this experience, cannot be made by top brass and imposed from above. It rises from the ranks. Each partisan is his own general. Partisan strategy is pragmatic and flexible, and thus hard to come by. Armies under a central command may win or lose. When they lose, it is over for them. But for every partisan contingent that goes down, a new one arises, as long as there are people. The partisan system, decentralized and enormously complex, turned out to be more stable than the relatively simple and highly centralized military system. The partisan system thrives on adversity and enhances a spirit of self-imposed sacrifice where the army system suffers demoralization. The partisan system is economical. There are no overhead expenses and no supervisory costs. There is no bureaucracy while the cost of military bureaucracy is skyrocketing.

One could continue, but it is clear that the partisan system was a self-management system applied to war—and it worked in Yugoslavia as it later did in Algeria, in Israel as in Vietnam, and in Malaysia as in Latin America.

The impact of technology on the disintegration of work and its regiments is perhaps less dramatic but in the long run it is no less radical.

The beginning of this process lies in the past. Lewis Mumford was one of its earliest and most prophetic observers. In 1934, in *Technics and Civilization,* he described how, on the one hand, power production and automatic machines tend to eliminate the regiments of blue-collar workers. Two million workers were cast out between 1919 and 1929 in the United States while production itself actually increased. And the displacement of the work force from the primary sector of production to the tertiary (often pseudo) sector of services continues apace. On the other hand, advance in technology, as it decreases the number of human robots in the plant, increases the number of trained technicians in the laboratories. This Mumford called, "the displacement of the proletariat."

The qualities of the new worker, as described by Mumford, are "alertness, responsiveness, an intelligent grasp of the operative parts: in short he must be an all-round mechanic rather than a specialized hand.

. . . With complete automation, freedom of movement and initiative returns for that small part of the original working force now needed to operate the plant."

Mumford foresaw the "stimulation of invention and initiative within the industrial process, the reliance upon group activity and upon intimate forms of social approval, and the transformation of work into education, and of the social opportunities of factory production into effective forms of political action."

He predicted decentralization as a potential consequence of the new technologies: "Bigger no longer automatically means better: flexibility of the power unit, closer adaptation of means to ends, nicer timing of operation, are the new marks of efficiency in industry." This process of decentralization, however, need not be anarchical or uncoordinated.

"Small units of production can nevertheless be utilized by large units of administration, for efficient administration depends upon record-keeping, charting, routing, and communication, and not necessarily upon a local overseership."

But all these advances toward decentralization and a humanly controlled and effectively directed industrial production "await the formulation of non-capitalist modes of enterprise."

Mumford in fact predicted the abandonment of the concept of private ownership of natural resources. "The private monopoly of coal beds and oil wells is an intolerable anachronism—as intolerable as would be the monopoly of sun, air, running water . . . and the common ownership of the means of converting energy, from the wooded mountain regions where the streams have their sources down to the remotest petroleum well, is the sole safeguard to their effective use and conservation." Here are all the elements of the contemporary theories of self-management, including the concept of social ownership which is the basis of Yugoslav theory.

SOCIAL OWNERSHIP

In Yugoslavia, self-management took off from a socialist background after a phase of expropriations and nationalizations. In other countries, this background does not exist. Must they go through socialism—Marxist or other—in order to get self-management, or can self-management be established in the context of private ownership and a capitalist production system?

Some of the participants at the Center conference, especially those from the United States and Great Britain, answered affirmatively. However, the experience from which they drew was more of a socio-psychological than a socioeconomic nature and was restricted to very small-scale and isolated systems of operation. Self-management, in fact, may be many things to many people. It may be a public-relations gimmick; it may be a means to get more out of the workers and to cut cost; it may be a mental health medicine; it may be a research project, an experiment, a revolution.

One of the editors of this book, Ichak Adizes, points out in his portion that far more important than ownership is the "sharing of managerial prerogatives." He goes so far as to assert that "social ownership in Yugoslavia is a barrier to the future development of self-management rather than a basis for it, because it hampers the mobility of labor and it hampers the mobility of capital."

Another participant in this selection, Einar Thorsrud, points out that in his country, Norway, self-management was introduced both in publicly and privately owned companies, and "when it comes to the mechanisms of workers' participation, the roles of people on the boards are exactly the same."

All these positions have one point in common: they indicate what is explicit also in Yugoslav theory, that self-management is a process that moves on a different plane from that of ownership. Self-management, in fact, articulates relations among people much more than relations between people and things. Therefore, what is important is not that the worker should own resources or the means of production but that nobody else should own them and thereby be placed in a position of hiring and firing and otherwise directing and manipulating the workers. If self-management need not be based on workers' ownership, it certainly excludes the possibility of ownership by others. The Yugoslav concept of social ownership in fact is a negative concept. It is the negation of ownership.

THE DISINTEGRATION OF PRIVATE PROPERTY

The disintegration of ownership is another one of the irresistible trends of contemporary history that moves modern societies in the direction of self-management.

I can distinguish three major developments tending to disintegrate our classical ownership concept. All three are interconnected.

Areas Beyond the Limits of Ownership Rights

First, technology is opening up new areas which are presently beyond the limits of ownership rights, whether of private individuals or of states (sovereignty), and to which the concept of ownership simply is not applicable. These include the limitless expanse of outer space and the depth of ocean space, which international law defines as "the common province of mankind" and "the common heritage of mankind" respectively. According to internationally accepted principles, these areas cannot be appropriated by any state or person, whether individual or corporate. They must be managed with the participation of all nations on equal terms and for the benefit of mankind as a whole, with particular regard to the needs of developing peoples. Here is the principle of nonappropriability, the negation of ownership writ large.

Environment

The second factor is the rise of environmental concern. This, again, has a strong technological component, but it also has a Weltanschauung component. It reflects a less anthropocentric view of man in his environment and a new reverence for nature, of which we are part.

Be this as it may, the social control of our environment and the improvement of its quality impose restrictions on private-property rights which mankind, in the laissez-faire period of capitalist expansion, did not know and would not accept.

Now there is a clear and open conflict between unrestricted private ownership and social environmental control. You can have either one or the other. Political development during these last few years and the impact of the Stockholm conference on the human environment seem to indicate that, with a heavy heart and many misgivings, mankind will be moving in the direction of a socially controlled environment and the disintegration of private ownership, as we have legally perceived it until now.

Resources

Resource management, of course, is the key to environmental control.

Current views on the earth's natural resources range from one extreme to the other. Whatever the position one takes, however, all resources must follow the way of ocean and outer-space resources, that is, they must be declared the common heritage of mankind.

If one accepts the position that resources are scarce, that heedless overexploitation and the goal of unlimited growth will, in the imminent future, exhaust all available energy sources, despoil mineral reserves, deforest continents, erode soils, deplete stocks, and drain water supplies, then the time has come, and is in fact overdue, when resources are too precious to be left to the whims of a market economy and the destructiveness of competitive private management. Rational resource management must be socially controlled—and this, certainly, undermines the concept of private ownership of resources as we know it. "The private monopoly of coal beds and oil wells is an intolerable anachronism—as intolerable as would be the monopoly of sun, air, running water. . . ."

If, on the other hand, one takes the position that the end of one phase of human economy is only the beginning of another; that the age of fossil fuel energy will be followed by the age of unlimited fusion energy; that the steel age will be followed by the magnesium age; that technology, through synthesis and mega-cycling, will produce unlimited resources, then natural resources lose their economic value. There is no more rent in them. To "own" them would be not so much intolerable as meaningless—as meaningless as to own the water of the oceans or the light of the sun. Resources in the post-industrial era will become common property as they were in the preindustrial and precapitalist era, in which they were (or appeared to be) equally unlimited.

WEALTH-PRODUCING FACTORS

The third development which is undermining our classical concept of ownership and property, then, is a shift that has been taking place in the weight of wealth-producing factors. Wealth is the product of resources, capital, and labor, with labor being divisible into manpower and skill. Skill used to be only one of the factors and by no means the most important, but technological advances keep increasing its significance. Skill, know-how, education, and organization, however, are not "owned" by anybody. They are the common heritage of mankind.

The social order toward which we are moving therefore does not depend on expropriations. It does not transfer ownership rights from one group or class of people to another, nor from private owners to the state. It simply disintegrates and negates the concept of ownership. In such an order there are neither owners nor nonowners, therefore neither employers nor employees. There always will be more skilled and less skilled, better-educated and less-educated members in any working society. But in a social order not based on property but on self-management, this division need not be static. Such a working society is a learning society in which the unskilled worker is motivated to spend a great deal of his time on learning—learning to participate meaningfully in the making of decisions affecting his work and his environment. Every worker is a manager, and everyone who starts at the bottom may end, or, rather, have his turn, at the top. There is in fact no top and no bottom, self-management being a process that feeds back on itself.

A working society that is a learning society is also one that accelerates the process of development. This has been the experience in country after country. A recent seminar on profit-sharing and joint management which was held in Cairo, with delegates from nine developing nations, came to conclusions very similar to those reached by the Center seminar on self-management. "Many countries of the world are currently engaged in the task of promoting rapid economic development with a view to providing rising standards of living to their peoples," the Cairo seminar stated in its final report. "This task involves a revolutionary transformation of their social and economic institutions and a reorientation of the attitudes of their peoples. As a consequence, in the field of economic activities they are required to create new forms of organization and devise innovative methods of operating enterprises irrespective of the nature of their ownership."

Self-management building may conflict with nation building in the new and developing nations insofar as the nation is identified with the centralized state of modern European history, while the thrust of self-management is decentralizing and de-statizing. It is likely, however, that this identification of nation and centralized state will turn out to be at fault, not self-management. A self-managing, decentralized economy is likely to turn out to be more viable in the face of environmental stresses and the threat of penetration by more developed Western economies than is a centralized, state-controlled one.

"In this context and in the light of problems and practices examined by the delegates," the Cairo report concludes, "the seminar came to the view that there was an overwhelming necessity of developing a new approach to management of enterprises which recognizes the importance of achieving higher levels of productivity. The seminar regarded profit-sharing and joint management as one of the most effective means of creating necessary conditions and motivations for this purpose. . . ."

WORLD ORGANIZATION AND SELF-MANAGEMENT

In summary, the impact of technology on the organization of war and peace, as well as the disintegration of ownership, caused by our penetration of spaces beyond the limits of ownership rights, by environmental and resource pressures, and by a shift in the relative weight of wealth-producing factors, are facets of a universal experience of the late twentieth century. They make the Yugoslav experience with self-management potentially universal.

There is another universal experience, working in the same direction. This again has two dialectically complementary components. For there are two forces working within the human universe: one centrifugal, the other centripetal—integrative and disintegrative forces—and in this system, under the impact of these forces, a continuous regrouping and reclustering is taking place.

For a few hundred years, we have been living in era of nation-states. We have been living in a hierarchical, vertical order; in a closed order, based on property, power, and sovereignty; in an order dominated by Western, Judeo-Grecian-Roman values.

Now we are regrouping. We are going to live in a postnational era in which nations will still exist but they will no longer be the sole actors, or even the protagonists, on the scene of world history, because other interests and other forms of organization—economic and cultural—are taking their place alongside and across the nation-state. We will live in a horizontal order, where men again participate in the decisions affecting them; we will live in an open order, with every person being a part of a number of overlapping subsystems organizing his work, leisure, economic life, cultural and spiritual life, and moving freely within these subsystems; and we will live in an order based no longer on property, nor on power, nor on sovereignty, for all these concepts are eroding under our eyes.

Finally, we will live in an order no longer dominated by Judeo-Grecian-Roman values. The new life-style will be infused with an admixture of Oriental values—symbolized by the dramatic entry of China into world organizations.

Owing to the working of the centrifugal force, there is today a remarkable tendency within nation-states to break up. This is a worldwide trend, affecting developed as well as developing nations, East, West, South, and North. I have only to mention Northern Ireland or Croatia, or Katanga or Nigeria, or East Bengal or Quebec, and it becomes clear what is meant. The black power movement in the United States should be viewed in the same context—as should, for that matter, student power, or even woman power.

What is remarkable is that the forces of law and order, sophisticated and formidable or even hypertrophized though they may be, are increasingly less capable of coping with these internal-disintegrative movements, just as, externally, they are impotent in the face of even weak and undeveloped antagonists, as in Vietnam.

Each of these movements has of course its own physiognomy, its own roots in its own history, and its own goals. What they have in common, however, is an urge toward self-determination, self-management, participation in decision-making on a scale that is comprehensible in human terms.

Self-managing and self-governing communities, whether of a cultural, national, racial, economic, or other character, will be much more important as the infrastructure of world order than they have been in the era of the centralized nation-state.

If the centrifugal force thus undercuts the power of the nation-state, the centripetal overcuts it. I am thinking of such developments as the multinational corporations, the European Economic Communities, the emerging ocean regime. Pressure comes from all these sectors of human activity which science and technology have so enlarged that they transcend the boundaries of the traditional nation-state. Resource and energy management, whether maritime or terrestrial, space technology, the management of the environment, weather control and modification, and transport and communications are cases in point. They have been dealt with in my previous studies, *The Ocean Regime* and *The World Communities.* For the purpose of this discussion it may be enough to remember the following points:

(1) The international institutions apt to cope with these problems are not primarily or directly based on nation-states nor are they an addition or merger of nation-states; they arise from transnational, non-territorial functions.

(2) Each one of these functions is polyvalent and involves new forms of decision-making in which industry, science, and government must share.

(3) They are overlapping and interlocking.

(4) The overall structure containing these functions will not be a super-state with the appendages of territoriality and sovereignty, but a network of communities partly functional and partly political; partly governmental and partly nongovernmental; partly international and intranational, with the traits of government, a business, an enterprise, a cooperative, and a union.

The impact of the forces of integration and disintegration, then, may shape a world order in which the macro-organization of the interacting world communities, the median organization of the interacting self-governing nations (no longer states in the traditional sense), and the micro-organization of the self-managing enterprise or other subnational system will be based on the same principles so that each part reflects the whole and the whole reflects each part.

HUMAN NATURE

The forces of integration and disintegration acting on the human universe do not, however, stop at the level of the self-managing subsystems. They affect each individual; rather, our concept of human nature and our concept of world order are always based on the same principles and reflect each other.

Although we are by no means "beyond freedom and dignity," nor do we wish or expect to get there, it is clear that when we say we are free we are mostly kidding ourselves, such is the impact of our environment, the culture in which we live, our economic status, the kind of stimuli we are exposed to from the moment of conception onward, not to speak of our genetic heritage. Man is not really an individual, but a network of interacting forces, a shifting nodal point of influences. Statistically we can really whittle him down to nonexistence.

It is in his interaction with environmental forces and influences, though, that man gains his autonomy, he develops his responsibility and creates a freedom that does not preexist and must be recreated continuously.

His self-awareness increases with his awareness of his environment, both physical and social. Increasing awareness engenders increasing interaction, which in turn reintegrates his own structure and renders him autonomous, just as the self-managing subsystem creates and recreates its autonomy by interacting in the participatory structures of the wider community, just as the nation creates and recreates its sovereignty by interacting in the network of world communities.

A self-management theory, therefore, contains elements for an ideology for postindustrial man. It is an ideology which transcends the dualistic concept of man versus society; it abolishes the dichotomy between owner and nonowner, manager and worker, manual work and intellectual work, work and learning, work and leisure. It is an ideology which adapts to change, and enhances the growth and development of the individual, the society, the economy. It is also an ideology which offers an alternative to the corporate structure, decreases the power of bureaucracy, and deinstitutionalizes and humanizes. It is a practical philosophy which is embodied and enacted in a growing number of countries whose experience is there for us to learn from.

SELF-MANAGEMENT:
New Dimensions to Democracy

1

ON SELF-MANAGEMENT: AN ORGANIZATIONAL DEFINITION, A TYPOLOGY OF VARIOUS EXPERIMENTS IN THE WORLD AND A DISCUSSION OF THE ROLE OF PROFESSIONAL MANAGEMENT

by Ichak Adizes
Associate Professor, Graduate School of Management
University of California, Los Angeles

INTRODUCTION

SELF-GOVERNMENT, self-management, industrial democracy, cultural democracy, community organizations, participative systems—these terms are repeatedly used in various academic and political meetings. Yugoslavia is attempting to apply self-management (self-government) on a national scale; the Israeli from the beginning of this century have experienced community organizations and various forms of cooperation with the *kibbutz* and *Moshav* movements; Peru, from the late 1960s, has been involved in developing industrial communities; and the Scandinavian countries have taken several steps toward industrial democracy. Germany, France, Tanzania, Algeria, Egypt, the United States—East and West, developed and developing—all have made one or more changes in their economic or organizational structures to facilitate increased participation in decision-making. It appears that we are witnessing a global movement.

How are the concepts of industrial democracy, self-management, and participative systems related to each other, if at all—and if related, what do they have in common? What mechanisms do they employ, how do they differ from other conceptual systems? Can any conclusions (even tentative)

3

be drawn from a classification of the various attempts to increase participation around the world? What is the role of professional management and the unique facets of its behavior in participative or democratic organizations?

My aims in this paper are first, to clarify the concept of self-management, as I understand it from an organizational and systemic point of view; second, to compare it to other participative and non-participative systems; third, to classify the various attempts for increased participation around the world; and fourth, to analyze the role and behavior of professional management in the systems that call for increased participation of workers in decision-making.

THE CONCEPTS AND THEIR MEANINGS

I distinguish between the concepts of participation, democracy, and self-management as follows:

(1) Participation refers to the process of making decisions;

(2) Democracy is an institutionalized equal-opportunity process of decision-making within which participation takes place; and

(3) Self-management means an asymptotic attempt for direct and comprehensive, industrial, cultural and political democracy.

Accordingly, a system might be participative but not necessarily democratic if there is no organizationally institutionalized, legally recognized, equal opportunity for participation for all the arties that are affected by the decision made. Furthermore, a system could be democratic but not self-managed if the democracy is only extended to a portion of the system (like political democracy) and if it is based exclusively on representation. Self-management extends democracy to all endeavors of society and attempts to nurture this process via direct participation, minimizing representation as much as possible. Since representation cannot be eliminated but only reduced, I used the word "asymptotic" in my definition above. The emphasis on direct participation highlights the decentralized nature of self-management, as decentralization is not necessarily an integral component of democracy in general.

Participation

Formal participation in the process of decision-making can be measured by the legal rights one has to make decisions throughout the planning process. The planning process consists of determining goals, designing policies and strategies to achieve them, and making tactical decisions on utilization of means. The lowest level of formal participation is one which entitles the participant to determine the utilization of means; at a higher level, the individual or the group whose participation we are measuring legally participates in the design of policies and strategies. The highest level of participation is attained when one is entitled to determine systems goals.

These measurements of participation can be applied to mezzo and macro levels of society. On the mezzo[1] level (organizational level) we can measure, as defined above, the legal managerial prerogatives of various inputs in the production process (labor, capital and natural resources) in decision-making. First is the labor input. Systems tike the Yugoslav one have allocated to labor, i.e., to all the people with permanent membership in the organization, full and exclusive legal prerogatives of decision-making in determining goals, designing strategies, and utilizing means.

Capital, as an input for the production of outputs, is defined in this paper as accumulated net savings invested. In the United States capital entitles the investor in economic enterprises to legal managerial prerogatives in determining goals, strategies, and means via the private ownership prerogative concept. In centrally planned economies where the government appoints management and determines goals, strategies, and means, the government has almost the exclusive and all-inclusive right to participate. "Outsiders" to the membership of the organization make the decisions. The government might claim it represents labor, but since the *actual* labor in the organization has no participative rights, I perceive labor as having no institutional direct prerogatives of decision-making, just as they have none in capitalist systems. Thus, as far as my definition of labor is concerned, that is, as an input into the production process and its institutionalized prerogative to participate, I do not distinguish between centrally-planned and market economies. On the other hand, although the Yugoslav system considers accumulated savings within an organization as "past labor," I will nevertheless consider the Yugoslav case as one that does not recognize the contributors of capital as privileged to participate since the ideology negates the absentee ownership concept with its accompanying prerogatives of decision-making.

Natural resources are the third type of input into the production process, in addition to labor and capital. They include the air, water, and the land with its minerals or other non-man-made resources that took a prolonged time to be created, accumulated, or shaped. Their rate of exploitation at a given point in time expresses the rate of exchange between the benefits to be derived by various generations.

For reasons whose analysis is beyond the scope of this paper, some natural resources, especially most water and all air, have never been subject to the ownership of any individual or institution. They "belong" to the past, present, and future generations of society. This is "social ownership" in the generic sense of the word.

In capitalist society, where formally the decision-making prerogatives are based on the concept of ownership, natural resources are not represented in the organizations since no one owns them. Similarly, no one represents labor since it does not own anything in the organization either. It is expected that the interest of natural resources will be represented by the market forces, like labor interests are to be expressed in the market via supply and demand. In centrally planned economies the government represents social interests since it is expected to take into consideration the comprehensive socioeconomic goals of society. The result is, however, similar. In both systems natural resources per se (as is the case with labor) are not represented on the mezzo level of decision-making and as a matter of fact, no system gives them recognition in terms of managerial prerogatives.

There are some changes taking place however. In Western Germany's system of codetermination, labor, in addition to capital, has legal, institutional representation on managerial boards. Such a representation has been established in Peru as well. Ralph Nader in the United States has recommended consumer representation on the boards of directors, which might be the first step towards the representation of environmentalists as well. In general, however, triple representation with institutional managerial prerogatives of all the production inputs does not yet exist.

We will next consider macro measurements of participation. On the macro level three macro subsystems will be distinguished. First is the Economic subsystem which is comprised of organizations geared to material goals, measured by (economic) output/input. The goal of these organizations is primarily to increase the net balance of their material resources. These organizations are either production (asset)-based like steel factories, or human capital (service)-based like insurance or banking corporations.

Second is the Sociocultural and Welfare subsystem. This subsystem is comprised of organizations in the arts, education, and health. They are geared to human capital improvement and are guided primarily by a human-social rationale to improve the process in which they are involved for the sake of improving the process. Economic, materialistic viability is a constraint and not a goal (the opposite of the economic subsystem, where the human process is probably the constraint while economic viability is the goal).

The third subsystem I wish to identify at the macro level is the Ideological subsystem. This subsystem is comprised of institutions that deal with and facilitate national and local level decision-making based on certain ideological concepts. The government and political parties are the functional vehicles of this subsystem. Their goal, I suggest, is the acquisition and maintenance of power; they are guided primarily by a power-play rationale dependent upon economic viability and on the effect it will have on social processes. Thus what are deterministic goals for the economic and social subsystems by my definition are only constraints for the political ideological subsystem.

The three subsystems have different goals and rationales for achieving them. The goals are by definition in conflict at any given point in time (although in the long run they are means to each other). Because of this conflict, at any point in time if one subsystem dominates and subverts other subsystems to operate according to its rationale, the society in general will not necessarily attain its comprehensive socioeconomic and political goals.

The economic, sociocultural, and political subsystems participate formally or informally in the macro decision-making process. Their participation can be conceptually measured the way it is measured for the mezzo inputs (labor, capital, and natural resources). The degree of participation of each subsystem can be determined by the legal rights and organizational capability of each in affecting the employment of means, design of strategies, and determination of goals on the macro scale, i.e., its strength in affecting legislation, economic and social policies, and national budgets.

Only Yugoslavia has legally institutionalized the participation of all three subsystems in macro decision-making. They have an economic chamber of the Parliament that is comprised of representatives of industry who legislate regulations pertaining to the economic endeavors of society. They also have a sociowelfare chamber composed of representatives from educational and health institutions that legislate in the sociocultural and welfare field. Other systems rely exclusively on the political subsystem to be the exclusive vehicle for institutionalized participation in decision-making. They expect the politicians to take into account in their decision-making the interests of the economic and sociocultural institutions. Analyzing the institutional participative patterns, it could be concluded then that in all systems except self-management the representation and prerogatives of decision-making are legally and formally afforded to one or at most two inputs (labor and/or capital) in the production process for the mezzo level of society and that they all rely on the political subsystem for identifying the comprehensive socioeconomic goals of society.

Democracy

Democracy was defined above as an institutionalized equal-opportunity process of decision-making within which participation takes place. I have suggested how to measure participation for micro inputs on the mezzo level of society and for the various subsystems on the macro level of society.

Accordingly, democracy in the political subsystem means that each citizen has an equal opportunity to participate in decision-making, provided in an institutionalized way via a political machinery. In the economic subsystem "the vote" or capability to participate is of a different nature than in the political subsystem. It is expressed in economic terms via a monetary common denominator like "the Dollar." The stronger an entity is, as expressed in its assets, earnings, and competitive power, the stronger is its role in the economic sphere. Thus, the higher the economic concentration in the economic subsystem, the less "democratic" it will be.

On the mezzo level, if labor does not have an equal opportunity to participate and as a matter of fact if it has no institutional channels of participation within the organization but has to act as a pressure group, as "outsiders," the decision-making process is not democratic.[2] It is rather hierarchical, secured in the hands of management who formally and legally represent capital. The vote here is also based on the economic entity of "the dollar invested." Consequently, although a system can be politically structured to be democratic, the process of participation in the economic subsystem can be hierarchical and nondemocratic.

Thus, when talking about democracy, one must distinguish very clearly the specific subsystem boundaries within which it prevails.

Self-Management

Self-management or self-government—concepts which to me are identical—means a direct comprehensive democracy which encourages democracy in the economic, political, and cultural subsystems and which affords to all participants in the production process democratic representation for participation.

To further illustrate the basic conceptual and methodological differences between the self-management, the market mechanism, and the state (centrally planned) systems, I present below the different conceptual models on which they operate.

COMPARING THE SELF-MANAGEMENT MODEL TO THE MARKET AND STATIST MODELS

Both market economies and centrally planned state economies have a conceptual framework in common.[3] They assume that conflict is resolved *externally* to the organizations that operate within the system. Furthermore, the mezzo organizations in both systems are hierarchically structured, since only one group (capital or government) has the exclusive legal prerogatives of management.

As can be seen from the following charts, the two systems are not different from each other so far as their systems *framework* is concerned. They are mirror images. Both rely on *external* throughputs to each organization for resolution of conflicts that exist or are created by the fact that society has multiple, comprehensive goals rather than exclusive goals. Organizations in state economies rely on the state government to set and regulate sociopolitical and economic goals and priorities which are articulated in "The Plan." Organizations in market economies rely on "the market" to regulate organizational goals which in turn are expected to achieve comprehensive sociopolitical goals for the society. That the market, an independent objective mechanism, is expected to provide for comprehensive goals can be seen from the fact that a pure classical market economist rejects any government intervention, regulation, or planning of social functions and forces (see Chart 1).

We are becoming increasingly aware that these pure hierarchical systems are inadequately structured to respond to a changing environment. In fact, to correct the ineffectiveness of the pure market model, government has increased its regulatory powers in an attempt to increase the goal comprehensiveness of each organization so that they take into account social goals as well as economic goals.

In the centrally planned model also, the system called for some alterations. Each organization could conform to plans so long as most of the goals were economic in nature and so long as most of the economic growth was derived from structural changes in the transition from agriculture to heavy industry. Once productivity had to be derived from better organization, once economic growth became based on consumer goods where market uncertainty is higher than in industrialized goods, and once measurable economic goals became less important than social goals which are process-oriented rather than immediate-result oriented, the central government's capacity to plan for society started to experience difficulties. The centrally planned economies have already introduced "some" profit motivation (which in the future will necessarily lead to decentralization in decision-making), thus introducing some degree of market mechanism in order to facilitate adaptation to changing socioeconomic conditions (see Chart 2).

In spite of these changes, however, neither system has altered the *basic conceptual framework* on which it relies. Both systems still rely on forces external to each organization whether it be the pure market, the regulated market, or the government, to resolve the conflicts which exist as a result of the comprehensiveness of societal goals. Furthermore, they leave the mezzo organizations hierarchically structured.

This reliance on mechanisms external to each organization has increased the power of government in all cases. As problems become more complex, more powers are given to government to solve them. But the increased burden on government has only increased the bureaucracy and increased the monopolization of decision-making of the political subsystem; thus there is a further increase in the complexity of the situation since governments are not necessarily as flexible in adapting to change as changing conditions require them to be. This increased complexity, in turn, requires a further strengthening of the government, which finds it increasingly difficult to resolve in a democratic participative way that which it is called upon to resolve. Thus, both systems have failed to provide an institutionalized mechanism to resolve the increasing emergence of conflicts generated by the intensity of modern environments without endangering democracy as they respectively define it.

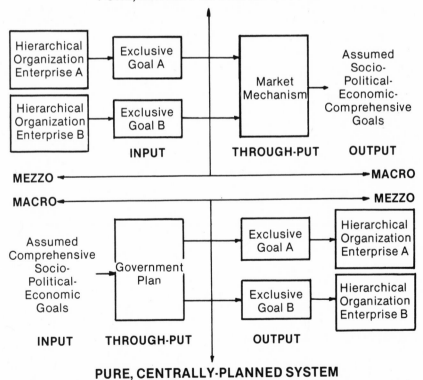

PURE, MARKET-ECONOMY SYSTEM

PURE, CENTRALLY-PLANNED SYSTEM

Chart 1. *Comparative Pure Systems*

Both systems, furthermore, are exclusively dominated by only one macro subsystem (although the respective subsystem is different for each), thus retarding the possibility of achieving comprehensive social goals. The market system is geared to economic growth and thus mainly oriented to satisfy the goals of the economic subsystem, while centrally planned systems are dominated by the political-ideological subsystem aiming primarily at increasing power and its petrification.

I suggest that systems which evolved to maximize the goals of one subsystem can be expected to experience difficulty in achieving comprehensive goals which include the interests of other subsystems. Both systems assume that maximizing the objectives of one subsystem will necessarily yield the desired comprehensiveness of social-economic-political goals.

REGULATED MARKET SYSTEM

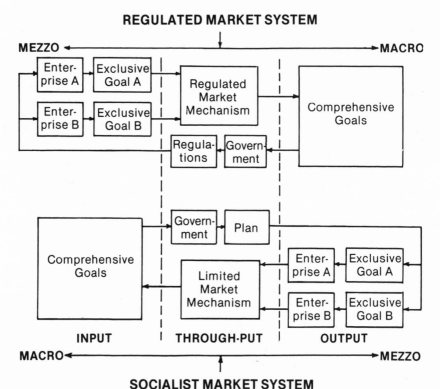

Chart 2. *Decentralized vs. Regulated Systems*

The self-management system (see Charts 3, 4) is fundamentally different from the two systems described above because it does not rely exclusively on the environment external to each organization to resolve conflicts created by the multiplicity of social goals. On the mezzo level, self-management provides for comprehensive goal achievement by enabling democratic participation of the various inputs in decision-making and by linking them to democratic macro institutions through the multiple role of each individual. It relies on institutionalized decentralization, and both the responsibility and the authority for resolving conflicts within and between organizations rest with the organizations themselves. This cuts down on the magnitude of "conflict pollution" that either the market or the government is supposed to "clean up."

Self-management in its ideal form (as expressed here) enables conflict resolution via democratic voting among the elected representatives *within* each input. Conflicts *between* inputs are resolved on the managerial boards of each institution. Conflicts *within* social subsystems are resolved in the elections for the legislative chambers of these subsystems. Conflicts *among* subsystems are resolved in decisions the various chambers have to make together and in supervision of the executive branch.

The self-management system is thus based on a fish-scale concept where multiple conflicting interests are resolved institutionally both on the mezzo and macro levels via multiple "linking pin" membership. Each member of any community is a member in other communities as well. For instance, a factory worker may be on the communal board of his municipality. Since he has equal voting power in all the organizations of which he is a member, he can legally represent the interests of one community in the other. Thus, when a decision is made democratically in a factory, it is expected that comprehensive goals will be sought. The same fish-scale conflict resolution model is institutionalized on the macro level.

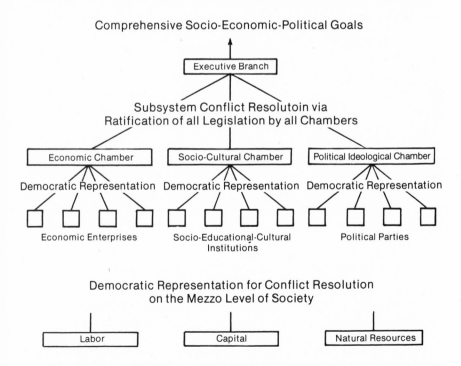

Chart 3. *Ideal Self-Management*

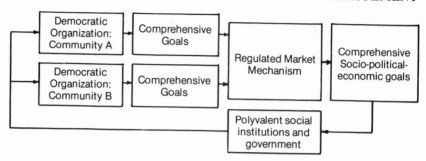

Chart 4. *Self-Management*

The multiple-chamber arrangement of the elected government and the fact that a political party no longer functions as the exclusive vehicle for multiple interest representation enable current conflict resolution on the basis of issues. Since each representative is responsible to the community that sent him, and is still employed by that community while a delegate, his loyalty is expected to be to the community whose interests he represents, and not to the political party. Since each chamber legally represents interests of subsystems, comprehensive social goals can be achieved since each interest gets equal power and authority and is linked not to a party but to the interests of the community. In a party system, economic powers (business) or political ideology (any) could take over the vehicle and thus deny the other subsystems an equal chance to effectuate comprehensive social goals.

In self-management in its ideal form, political, economic, and socio-cultural institutions have equal power and an institutional framework to resolve their conflicting interests or perceptions of reality. No one of them should be able to significantly subordinate the other. In other systems this is not the case, and from a systems point of view they are not *comprehensively* democratic.

Organizational (Mezzo Level) Meaning of Self-Management

In the self-management system equilibrium is sought among three subsystems: the authority (power and influence) subsystem, the task subsystem, and the reward subsystem. The characteristics of the equilibrium among the three subsystems are described as follows:

(1) The Authority-Power-Influence subsystem: the Authority-Power-Influence for making decisions should be distributed equitably among all constituents of society (or members of the organization), negating monopolization of decision-making prerogatives. Such a monopoly exists in alternative systems. In capitalist industrial organizations the legal prerogatives of decision-making are concentrated in the hands of the owners; labor does not have representation on the managerial levels of decision-making. Furthermore, economic institutions (macro level) have a stronger-than-desirable influence in political and cultural subsystems. In bureaucratism and technocratism on the other hand managerial prerogatives are concentrated in reality in the hands of those who possess

the information and manipulate the rest of society or organizations in making decisions suitable to those holding the information (the industrialized countries might be moving towards bureaucratization and technocratization, into a new form of monopolization based on information rather than capital). In statist, centrally planned systems, managerial prerogatives are concentrated in the hands of an exclusive political party which claims a monopoly in understanding social interests.

In self-management as discussed above,[4] *all* inputs that generate outputs should have the legal right to participate in decision-making and should be capable of doing so in reality.

(2) The Task subsystem: in hierarchically structured systems (whether the Soviet system or the United States corporation), the higher one ascends in the organization, the greater one's authority to make important decisions and commitments, and thus the greater the responsibility. It is the president or chairman, whether of the business corporation or of the Communist party, who is expected to be responsible for the highest task there is—the survival of the system of which he is in charge.

Self-management reverses this hierarchical distribution of tasks. The total community is expected to be responsible for the highest task there is—its survival. The executive, administrative hierarchy has responsibilities but only those which are delegated to it by the community at large.

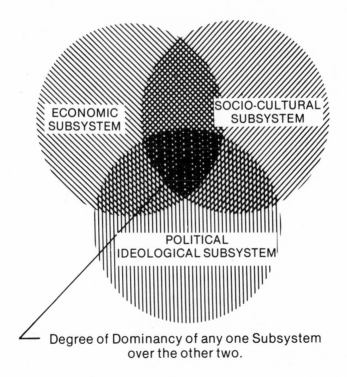

ECONOMIC SUBSYSTEM

SOCIO-CULTURAL SUBSYSTEM

POLITICAL IDEOLOGICAL SUBSYSTEM

Degree of Dominancy of any one Subsystem over the other two.

In balancing the task and authority subsystems in self-management, the organization or the society at large has the obligation to determine its survival strategy. For this task it has the ultimate authority, power, and influence to determine how this task should be interpreted and carried out, and suitable channels of participation should be provided to this effect.

In self-management the total community has the ultimate power and authority, total participation rights and capability, to effectuate its survival goals and strategies while in other systems it is usually vested in monopolistic or elitist groups of forces. In self-management, the greater the importance of the task, the greater should be the capability and right to participate and the greater should be the number of members of the system that should be participating in the decision, while in hierarchical organizations, the more important the decision, the smaller the number of people who make it.

(3) The Reward subsystem: the third element to be balanced in self-management is the distribution of rewards. Inequalities which exist in various imperfect systems (including imperfect market mechanisms) whereby various contributing inputs receive benefits which exceed their contributions (as assessed by other contributors) should be abolished. In other words, self-management wishes to abolish the inconsistency in rewards as related to the accomplishment of tasks and the contribution to social goals as perceived by the various parties involved.

Self-management seeks then to create conditions in which each participant (whether a human being or a producing or serving unit) of a system should make actual contributions by accomplishing tasks which lead to comprehensive socio-political-economic goals; have adequate authority, influence, and power to effectuate the expected contributions; have institutionally available channels to participate in the design of strategies and goals towards which those contributions are made; and receive rewards according to the objective value of the contributions made.

Goal: Authority = Tasks = Rewards

Authority   Task   Rewards
Power
Influence

Chart 5. *Subsystems in Self-Management*

The ultimate goal (see Chart 5), I believe, is that authority, power, and influence be derived from the task (professional authority as it is called in Yugoslavia) and the reward be mainly the intrinsic satisfaction of performing the task itself. This eliminates the distinction between physical and mental work, and it also eliminates the exclusivity of materialistic satisfaction as the goal for which society exists (eliminating profit motivation as the sole purpose of organizations). The three subsystems will then be fully integrated.

THE STRUCTURE AND BEHAVIOR OF MEZZO LEVEL ORGANIZATIONS IN SELF-MANAGEMENT AND ALTERNATIVE SYSTEMS

Community vs. Enterprise

I have defined self-management as a system of organizing society both on the macro and mezzo levels. In this next section, I contrast a self-managed organization (community) with an enterprise. The community is the organizational structure of self-management on the mezzo level, while an enterprise is the mezzo level organization of alternative systems, whether market or centrally planned economies. I will analyze the differences between communities and enterprises (in this paper I will concentrate on the market system based enterprise) since these two organizations are different by definition in structure and in behavior. Examples of communities are the Yugoslav self-managed enterprise, the Israeli kibbutz, and the Peruvian industrial community.

A community is defined in this paper as a group of people living in close association, having equal rights in determining their goals and course of action, and sharing the output of their efforts according to rules predetermined by them. Labor is both the producing input and the owner of the results of its work.

An enterprise on the other hand is an organization which conglomerates labor, capital, and natural resources and is primarily geared towards the achievement of economic results as measured by economic indices, such as the rate of return on investment, profits in absolute terms, profit margin on sales, etc. In a capitalist enterprise, goals are determined by management within constraints, one of which is labor. Labor, according to this definition, is mainly an input into the production process and as such is treated as a commodity that has a price in the market. The economic rewards for work done are determined mainly via the market mechanism as perceived by management.

AN ORGANIZATIONAL STRUCTURE OF AN ENTERPRISE

The customary organizational system as treated by theoretical economics can serve as an example of an enterprise. People work in order to produce economic results for which they are paid. The economic results achieved by the company should be sufficient to pay for the human contributions and capital investments when the cost of these contributions is basically determined by a competitive market in these commodities. If there is attention given to the human element in an enterprise, it is primarily to induce higher productivity rather than for the sake of seeking this element as a goal in itself. It is assumed that the social life of the members of each organization is their own concern, and the enterprise does not seek to provide, guide, or direct it.

In this structure, there are clear distinctions between labor, capital, and management. Management supposedly represents the total organization's long run interests and is expected to create a coalition of interests between labor and capital contributors as well as to take into account other interests or constraining factors such as government, consumers, and the society at large. Management provides leadership by acting as a catalyst that designs alternatives satisfactory to labor and capital, and distributes return on capital or labor investments in order to secure their continuing contribution. Management is mainly a mediating force representing the systemic interests of the total organization. Capital and labor continue to seek their own separate interests via bargaining with management. Prerogatives of management, that is, decision-making on the organizational goals and their implementation, are allocated to the managerial group which has the legal authority and the power to pursue these prerogatives.

In an enterprise, legal authority flows from the top down via the delegation process. A limitation to this authority is the level of acceptance by subordinates. Thus, one of the sources of managerial ability to implement decisions is its leadership capability.

THE ORGANIZATIONAL STRUCTURE OF A COMMUNITY

In a community, economic revenues are used as means to achieve a more comprehensive set of community goals. In line with the adage which says, "Eat to live, don't live to eat," a community produces in order to achieve a certain quality of life for its members rather than providing better social conditions in order to produce more and cheaper goods. For example, one may examine a community's reaction to stress from change. Assume that with environmental change some people are found to be dispensable. In an enterprise, if the legal constraints enable it, these people would be fired in the name of securing to owners a certain return on investment and would be left to seek employment elsewhere. The enterprise further assumes that the market mechanism will allocate the fired labor force to areas where they can serve best. The task of retraining is upon those fired or upon society in general. Thus, the enterprise employs to its best advantage what the society has to offer and considers contributions to society directly correlated with the magnitude of profits it generates in the long run. In a community, on the other hand, the responsibility for retraining labor or finding new opportunities for its employment is upon the community itself. This creates a sense of responsibility towards one another, even if it results in lowered profitability. Communities have to resolve their own problems rather than rely on external mechanisms for resolution.

Management in a community is elected and nominated by the members and is a part of them. It performs the role of administration by carrying out decisions made by the total membership to which it is legally responsible. Managerial prerogatives are mainly held by members of the organization, who may delegate these prerogatives to the managerial group (bottom up delegation rather than top down as in an enterprise).

Management's power is mainly limited to the powers necessary for implementation of decisions. Management has no exclusive discretion in making policy decisions of crucial importance to the well-being of the community. The authority for policy decisions rests exclusively with the community in general and cannot be relinquished.

Management performs the role of leadership by being responsible for presentation of alternative decisions for community approval. Once an alternative is selected, management performs the administrative role by implementing decisions. The idea is that the community in general is the master of its destiny. It determines its own goals and means and then works to realize them through its selected management.

In a community, the distinction between labor as a commodity and producing input, and labor as the owner of past labor (capital) and present results of its work, is blurred. External, loaned capital is treated as an input which constrains the community's discretion in decision-making the way labor constrains capital's decision-making in an enterprise.

Due to the ownership framework and the legal definition of the flow of authority, management does not determine the remuneration of the members of the community. The members themselves, through a democratic process, decide how to distribute the revenues whereby part of the distribution is their personal income.

In a community, workers do not feel themselves subordinate to management since legally they are equal members of the community, even though they perform different types of work. Subordination goes only so far as the implementation of a particular task requires and lasts only for the duration of time needed to accomplish the task. It is a subordination based on technological necessities and not of a universal and permanent nature. Since management is elected, the management is subordinate to the total membership which is free not to reelect it.

RELATIONSHIP TO SOCIETY OF A COMMUNITY AND OF AN ENTERPRISE

An enterprise, therefore, is an economic institution operating within a market system, providing economic outputs, and seeking economic efficiency and effectiveness. It derives its inputs from the social environment, and it is affected by it. However, its contribution to the social environment is mostly via the economic outputs of its operations.

A community, operating on the basis of both economic and social factors, contributes to the social environment directly. It is one of the cells of the social organism, and its goals are sociopolitical as well as economic in nature. A kibbutz, for instance, will consider artistic, cultural activity no less important than making profits. The same holds true for a Yugoslav factory that invests a substantial portion of its income in education, art, social activity, and recreation for its members, even if these activities are not immediately and necessarily related to increased productivity. In a community, social goals have their own justification.

A Comparison of Participative Systems

Various countries use different means in their attempts to increase participation and are somewhere between pure community and pure enterprise structure. Differences in these mixed systems are found in the scale of application, in the scope of the decisions in which participation is permitted, in the conceptual model applied so far as managerial functions are concerned, etc. The differences stem from the different problems the various countries try to solve via participation, and from the different sociopolitical and economic structures within which this participation is applied.

In Yugoslavia, the participative system applied (self-management) is viewed as a vehicle for the total transformation of society, towards decentralization of economic, political, and social activities. In the United States the aims are much less ambitious and much narrower in scope. The main goal appears to be increased productivity or improvement in the quality of working life. Retardation of centralization and democratization of society are not the explicit goals. The Peruvian Industrial Community, as another example, is attempting to afford a new, alternative approach to economic growth.

Participation thus appears to be a global answer for different needs. For developed nations, increased participation in decision-making appears attractive, for it improves the intrinsic rewards people get from their positions and tasks in the company. For developing nations it is a vehicle to stimulate higher productivity. For centralized systems, it appears to be a road to achieve a less bureaucratized, more democratic society. On the following pages, we will present the differences in the various systems' attempts to increase participation. The variables found in the different systems are described as follows:

(1) *Scale of application:* The systems vary from macro application (aimed at the whole society in its economic or social or political endeavors) like Yugoslavia, through mezzo application (increasing the level of participation within a single company) as in the United States, Britain, or Norway, to micro application (dealing with the self-realization of one individual as attempted in industrial psychology), found all over the world.

(2) *Comprehensiveness of implementation:* In certain countries such as Peru or Norway, the participative system is applied only to a subsystem (industry) or certain portions of it (univalent), while in Yugoslavia it is comprehensive and all-inclusive in nature (polyvalent), embracing economic, political, and sociocultural institutions.

(3) *Scope of participation:* In Yugoslavia and the Israeli kibbutz the scope is "the whole person." Participation extends from matters related to work, to the cultural and political life of the worker, and even to the management of the homes and neighborhoods he lives in.

In Norway and the United States where sociotechnical or other participative structures are employed, the scope of participation is mostly

THE DIFFERENCE BETWEEN AN ENTERPRISE
AND A COMMUNITY ORGANIZATIONAL TYPE:

Variable	*Enterprise*	*Community*
Goals:	Exclusively and mainly economic (for industrial organizations)	Comprehensive social, economic, political goals (for all organizations)
Social goals:	Means to economic goals	Goals in their own right
Legal authority to determine goals:	Legal owners, probably outsiders to the community, represented by management	The total membership of the community
Organization is legally a vehicle for:	The investor (owners)	The total community
Decision-making centers:	Primarily a state of centralization	Primarily a state of decentralization
Legal flow of authority:	Top down delegation	Bottom up and top down (circular) delegation
Distribution of managerial prerogatives:	Policy and administrative decisions made by professional management	Policy decisions made by total membership; administrative by professional management
Contribution to society:	Direct, mainly economic	Direct, economic-socio-political
Assumed environment:	Atomistic (competitive)	"Fish-scale" (cooperative)
Conflict resolution between inputs (capital and labor):	Via bargaining with management	Via consensus of the total community
Board of Directors representation:	Exclusively representatives of the owners or government, and mostly consisting of "outsiders"	Multiple interest representation accepted and mostly composed of "insiders"

limited to one's working place and time. In structures that do not even employ job enlargement, group tasks, etc., but rely only on profit sharing for increased participation, the scope of participation is even more limited and focused only upon the economic results.

(4) *Distribution of managerial prerogatives, mezzo level:* Legal managerial prerogatives are assigned to capital (in the United States), to labor (in Yugoslavia), to both (in Peru, Norway, West Germany), to capital, labor, and consumers (in the consumer-producer cooperatives). In the Israeli kibbutz the "entry ticket" into the system is a lifetime commitment to the organization. Since capital is past accumulated labor, lifetime commitment means future capital formation, and thus one conceptually commits both one's capital and one's labor.

(5) *Degree of pluralism sought, macro subsystems:* Various systems are designed to increase the pluralism of various macro-subsystems, thus seeking their better participation which subsequently should yield better decision-making in general. For example, economic decentralization in Yugoslavia or other Eastern European countries facilitated pluralism and mobility, which was expected to improve decision-making on economic endeavors and thus improve economic results.

(6) *Degree of pluralism sought, mezzo level inputs:* Whether the system is designed to encourage or discourage labor and capital participation, mobility will have an effect on the monopolies of power and on participation. A system can seek pluralism of its economic subsystem by decentralization (government relaxing its mandatory plans) while at the same time discouraging input pluralism, as in Yugoslavia where labor mobility is constrained by the system because individuals cannot enjoy future fruits of past investments once they move out of the company.

(7) *Magnitude of mandatory application:* In certain countries like the United States or Israel the application of a participative system of *any* nature is voluntary. In Yugoslavia and Peru the mechanism is prescribed by law, and any organization or individual that violates the system is subject to legal prosecution.

(8) *Concept of ownership employed:* I distinguish among four types of ownership—private, communal, state, and social. In this paper, ownership will mean one's legal right to use one's property according to one's choice and the right and capability to benefit from the future fruits of one's past investments embodied in this property.

Private property will thus mean one's right to utilize, within legal constraints, one's property and benefit from the fruits of this utilization.

Communal ownership will mean that the community, or the participative system under study, its total membership or its legal representatives decide on the utilization of the property and on the distribution of the fruits. Communal ownership is thus an extension of private property. It is basically the private property of several people who agree on how to use and benefit from the shared property, retaining the freedom to take their individual shares out.

State ownership is communal ownership on a larger scale where society is represented by the state the way the community is represented by elected representatives in deciding how to deal with the communal property. In state ownership, however, members of the community do not have the right to pull out their share—a departure from private property. Thus, state ownership, while related to the private ownership concept, is not an extension of it.

The *Social Ownership* concept is a total departure from any extension of private property. Resources which are social property do not belong to anyone but to society in general, which means in essence to no one and to everyone at the same time. There is no *single* institution that can claim that it legally represents the owners of the property. Those who work with these resources can benefit from the results of the use of those assets. However, they can only increase the resources overall and not decrease them. Once an individual quits the organization, he has no ownership rights over the past contributions he has made to increase these resources.

(9) *Management-labor differentiation:* Here we are faced with different conceptual frameworks. In Yugoslavia such differentiation is desiredly and theoretically eliminated. All members of the organization manage. The same holds true for the Israeli kibbutz or Moshav. In Peru, Norway, or in the United States experiments, the labor-management distinction is maintained.

(10) *Managerial appointments:* In Norway and the United States, managerial appointments are from the top down, and the general membership does not have a legal say in it. In Yugoslavia and the Israeli kibbutz, management is elected by the people who are going to be managed and no outside forces have any legal right in this decision.

(11) *Role of management:* In Yugoslavia, the kibbutz, the role of the executive, administrative branch has been significantly altered from what we are familiar with in hierarchical structures (see following pages). In the United States, Norway, and Germany the role of management remains what it was before the participative system was introduced, and only its attitude is expected to change.

(12) *Management tenure:* In Peru, Germany, Norway, and the United States there is no institutional rotation of management nor are there reelections. In Yugoslavia and the kibbutz each person in a managerial position is up for reelection and usually the office rotates between various members of the organization.

(13) *Conflict resolution mechanisms:* The mechanisms for resolving conflicts among the interests of the various inputs vary among the following: external-to-the-organization bargaining via external pressure groups or strikes, as in the United States; internal bargaining via labor representatives in joint management boards as in Germany; consensus voting of all membership involved, as in Yugoslavia or the Israeli kibbutz.

(14) *Representation on boards of directors:* Legal representation of capital only, of labor only, or representatives of both, in addition to other interest groups like the external consumers or producers in certain cooperatives, comprise representation on Boards of Directors. Board of

Directors in this connotation means the highest governing body. Workers Councils in Yugoslavia will be the Board of Directors by this definition.

(15) *Magnitude of participation encouraged:*

(a) *Authority to determine goals* is a reflection of the level of decentralization and magnitude of participation. Whether management or the total membership of the organization decides[5] what the organizational goals will be is significant for the flow of authority and location of responsibility.

(b) *Policy decisions* can be legally made by management or by the total organization membership. In the kibbutz and in Yugoslavia, for instance, policy decisions are made by the total membership or its elected representatives. The more important the decision, the more members ("lower" levels of the organizational structure) must be involved in it—just the opposite is expected in a hierarchical organization; there the more important the decision, the smaller the number of people involved in making it.

(c) *Administrative decisions* can be made by general membership or administrators.

(16) *Decision-making centers:* A hierarchical organization presumes that ultimate decision rights are concentrated at the top. When top management considers it of value, it might delegate some decisions downwards. The self-managed organization on the other hand assumes that all decisions are the responsibility of the constituents, who decide which decisions they *cannot* make collectively, and then delegate to their representatives the authority to make these decisions for them. The elected deputies are accountable for these decisions to the general membership. Thus, a distinction is made between institutionalized "top down" or "bottom up" organizations.

(17) *Assumed environment:* An atomistic-environment concept expects competitive forces to yield comprehensive socioeconomic political goals. This atomistic environment concept assumes that conflicts are resolved by mechanisms *external* to each organization. A fish-scale environment concept, on the other hand, recognizes confluency of interest groups and overlapping membership of various organizations. The fish-scale environment concept thus assumes that conflicts should be institutionally resolved *within* each organization. For instance, Galbraith's concept of countervailing power, by this distinction, is atomistic in nature, while Ralph Nader's demand that consumer representatives by put on Boards of Directors in the United States is based on a fish-scale concept.

(18) *Social goals and means:* Social goals can be means to economic goals. For instance, the human behavior approach in many organizations has been subverted not to forward social goals per se, but to provide better stimuli and conditions for higher economic productivity. In the self-management system, social goals are sought for themselves even though the system is conscious that they might be at the expense of economic goals. In self-management, participation facilitation is a goal in itself beyond the economic productivity it might yield.

THE DILEMMA OF PROFESSIONAL
MANAGEMENT IN SELF-MANAGEMENT

The Managerial Problems of Communities

A pure community structure or a participative structure may have advantages over the pure enterprises, but the success of a community will depend upon its capacity to resolve some serious managerial problems.

From my in-depth studies of the Yugoslav organizational system, from very close knowledge of the contemporary problems a kibbutz faces, and from an awareness of the issues with which the Peruvian Comunidad Industrial is struggling, I have derived some *insights* into the *common managerial* problems that communities have. In presenting those problems I will attempt to concentrate on the Yugoslav system, where they are more accentuated and present contrasts to Israel and Peru. The purpose of presenting these problems is to focus on those issues that need to be resolved and on the pitfalls that should be avoided if the development of communities is desired. These problems are not exclusive and generic only to communities. They might seriously hamper the effectiveness of enterprises as well. However, solving these problems is essential, a *sine qua non*, for the existence of a community, while for an enterprise these problems are only hindering factors.

PROBLEMS OF OWNERSHIP:
THE DILEMMA OF COMMITMENT VS. MOBILITY

In order to give legality to the management prerogatives of the total community, the frame of ownership has been a communal or social one, precluding managerial ownership rights to anyone not on the payroll of the company. In a kibbutz the total present and future membership owns the assets. In Yugoslavia, although the ownership of the fixed assets rests with the society in general, the members of the community have ownership rights to the results of their work. In the same way, only the members of a cooperative own a share of the company that they manage together. The Peruvian Comunidad Industrial owns a share of the company depending on the magnitude of its investments.

The perceived advantage of communal ownership is in concentrating the sources of managerial prerogatives into a community. The concept of communal ownership is supposed then to generate a spirit of common cause, common goal, and common interest.

The belief that commitment will be generated from ownership rights is based in my opinion on erroneous assumptions. In Yugoslavia, it was found that although everyone was an owner, not everyone was committed. A commitment, I suggest, results from a real opportunity to exercise managerial prerogatives.[6] Such a finding can be expected. If an owner has no way of affecting decisions made with his resources, he will not feel committed to the organization. On the other hand, managers who do not have ownership rights might be highly committed to the organization if it is a creation of their labors. In a community where the channels of decision-making are non-operative, where a clique of managers succeeds in

PARTICIPATIVE TYPOLOGY

VARIABLES — PARTICIPATIVE SYSTEMS	1 SCALE OF APPLICATION		2 COMPREHENSIVENESS OF PARTICIPATION		3 SCOPE OF PARTICIPATION			4 DISTRIBUTION OF INSTITUTIONAL MANAGERIAL PREROGATIVES		
	mezzo	macro	limited to	comprehensive socio-econ. politico	profits	work-production matters	whole scope	to capital	to labor	to others
Yugoslavia Self-management	X	X		X	X	X	X		X	
Norway Industrial Democracy	X		industry			X		X	X	
Peru Industrial Community	X		certain industry		X	X		X	X	
Germany Co-determination	X		industry		X	X		X	X	
U.S.A. Socio-tech; organiz. dev; participative organizations	X			X	X	X	very limited application	X		
Israel Kibbutz	X			X	X	X	X	X ipso facto	X	
Moshav ovdim	X			X	X	X			X	
Moshav shitufi	X			X	X	X	X		X	
Cooperatives (anywhere)	X		certain organizations		X	X		X	X	

(continued on facing page)

PARTICIPATIVE TYPOLOGY

PARTICIPATIVE SYSTEMS	5 MAGNITUDE OF PLURALISM SOUGHT -MACRO LEVEL			6 MAGNITUDE OF PLURALISM SOUGHT -MEZZO LEVEL			7 MAGNITUDE OF MANDATORY APPLICATION		8 CONCEPT OF OWNERSHIP				9 MGMT-LABOR—DIFFERENTIATION	
	econ.	socio-cultur.	political/ideological	product	capital	labor	manda-tory	volun-tary	pvt.	commu-nal	state	soc.	labor-mgmt. distinct	mgmt. equals labor
Yugoslavia Self-management	X	X		X	X	X	X		small X	small X		X		X
Norway Industrial Democracy	not intended			not intended			Wrkrs repre on Bds.	Ext. Appli-cation	X				X	
Peru Industrial Community	not intended			not intended			X		X	X			X	
Germany Co-determination	not intended			not intended			X		X				X	
U.S.A. socio-tech; organiz. dev; participative organizations	not intended			not intended				X	X				X	
Israel Kibbutz	not intended			not intended				X	very X ltd.			X		X
Moshav ovdim	not intended			not intended				X	X	X				X
Moshav shitufi	not intended			not intended				X	X	X				X
Cooperatives (anywhere)	not intended			not intended				X	X	X				X

(continued on overleaf)

PARTICIPATIVE TYPOLOGY

VARIABLES / PARTICIPATIVE SYSTEMS	10 MANAGEMENT APPOINTMENTS		11 ROLE OF MANAGEMENT		12 MANAGERIAL TENURE		13 CONFLICT RESOLUTION			14 BOARD OF DIR. OR EQUIV. REPRESENTATION		
	top down	bottom up	changed	unchngd	instit. rotation or re-elec.	no req'd. rotat. or re-elec.	external bargaining or strikes	labor vote on mgmt. boards	role of total membership	capital exclus.	labor excl.	multiple repres.
Yugoslavia Self-management		X	X		X				X		X	
Norway Industrial Democracy	X			X		X		X				X
Peru Industrial Community	X			X		X		X				X
Germany Co-determination	X			X		X		X				X
U.S.A. Socio-tech; organiz. dev; participative organizations	X			X		X	major X conflicts		minor X conflicts	X		
Israel Kibbutz		X	X		X				X		X	
Moshav ovdim		X	X		X				X		X	
Moshav shitufi		X	X		X				X		X	
Cooperatives (anywhere)		X	X		X				X			X

(continued on facing page)

PARTICIPATIVE TYPOLOGY

VARIABLES — PARTICIPATIVE SYSTEMS	15 MAGNITUDE OF PARTICIPATION ENCOURAGED FOR GENERAL MEMBERSHIP						16 DECISION MAKING CENTERS		17 ASSUMED ENVIRONMENT		18 SOCIAL GOALS, MAINLY	
	goal determin.		policy decisions		means							
	mgmt.	total member-ship	mgmt.	total member-ship	mgmt.	total member-ship	primary state of centr.	primary state of decen.	atomist	fish scale	means to econom.	goals in their own right
Yugoslavia Self-management		X		X	X			X		X		X
Norway Industrial Democracy	X		X		X		X			X	X	X
Peru Industrial Community	X		X		X		X			X	X	X
Germany Co-determination	X		X		X		X			X	X	
U.S.A. Socio-tech; organiz. dev; participative organizations	X		X	X		X	X		Is Pseudo X participative	X	Is Pseudo participative X	Organizational Development
Israel Kibbutz		X		X		X		X		X		X
Moshav ovdim		X		X		X		X		X		X
Moshav shitufi		X		X		X		X		X		X
Cooperatives (anywhere)		X		X		X		X		X		X

27

entrenching itself in positions of power, where the community members follow the democratic decision-making requirements as a ritual to rubber stamp management's decisions, the members will generally not have any commitment to a cause although they legally own the assets or results of their work. Furthermore, a relatively deeper sensation of frustration will prevail in a community than in an authoritatively-managed enterprise because of the disparity between the actual and the expected. The strikes in Yugoslav companies are symptomatic of such cases. Theoretically, there is no need to strike in Yugoslavia since the community can make the decisions it wishes. There is no need for pressure to be exercised via strikes to obtain certain benefits for any one group. Striking in Yugoslavia is an expression of dissatisfaction with a reality which does not comply with what was anticipated: "Democracy is only a camouflage for dictatorship—the establishment uses it to its own benefit. Major changes by the constituents are impossible to effectuate without disrupting the system . . ." might be a typical complaint of a Yugoslav striker (and similarly of the members of one American political community—the students in the colleges).[7]

Thus ownership alone does not necessarily lead to commitment and productivity. What is needed, rather, are channels of decision-making which enable all members to feel that they are contributing and that they can effectively master their immediate environment. This, however, is an extremely difficult managerial task to achieve, one which will be looked at in more detail in the next section. In an enterprise, by comparison, where workers do not necessarily expect to manage, alienation from this cause, I suggest, will be lower.

The disadvantages of the social type of ownership are even greater than in communal ownership, which, as we have seen, does not necessarily yield commitment. Social ownership also limits mobility. When an individual wants to leave the community, does he get a fair share of his investments? Can he benefit from the future fruits of his past sacrifices? In an enterprise this problem is easily resolved for the owners—they own shares which are marketable. The price of a share represents what the buyers judge to be the value of a company when it is computed in terms of future profits. These future profits are results of past decisions and sacrifices. Thus, an owner who wants to leave an enterprise through the selling of his share should be able to realize the future fruits of his past investments through the price for which he sells his stock.

This is not so in the Yugoslav enterprise, or the kibbutz, although it is possible in cooperatives. When a Yugoslav worker wants to leave a company, he takes nothing with him. In past years, he may have voted to reinvest profits rather than to distribute them as wage-bonuses. These past sacrifices do not bear any fruits to him in the future unless he stays on the company payroll. Social ownership thus might hamper labor and capital mobility which are necessary conditions for an effective market-oriented economy. In the Israeli kibbutz, this problem is not of major significance since people usually join kibbutzim with a lifelong commitment but in Yugoslavia, where labor and capital mobility are desired, this structure has its disadvantages.

Thus, the first insight to be gained from the Yugoslav experience is that communal *esprit de corps,* a sense of collective commitment to a cause, a feeling of mastering one's own destiny via potent participation and effective democratic processes, is not necessarily accomplished via communal or social ownership of assets. Social ownership, rather, might hamper labor and capital mobility which might be crucial for an economy that wishes market forces to operate in it. While there is no necessary relationship between commitment and ownership, there is, apparently, a positive relationship between one's opportunity to affect the conditions of the environment within which he operates, and the commitment he feels to those activities. Thus, instead of ownership, one should investigate managerial prerogatives and their adequate distribution throughout the total membership of the organization, i.e., community self-management.

THE COMMUNITY'S INVOLVEMENT IN DECISION-MAKING AND ITS PROFESSIONAL MANAGEMENT

In a community, a primary state of decentralization should exist. Tasks should be delegated to management for implementation via administration of the policy and strategic decisions made by the community in general. Management in a community should be directly responsible to the constituents who elect it. This state of affairs whereby management is in relative subordination to the people for whom it manages has a wide range of consequences. One consequence is potential management demoralization. Another one might be workers' disorientation and community disintegration. These results might stem from the community's excessive demand for control over its professional management.[8]

As a control mechanism, the community rotates its managers, requests them frequently to report their decisions, and rebuffs them for decisions which the community in its collective wisdom considers to be erroneous. Since the members of the organization belong to a relatively small community, management finds it hard to hide its mistakes. The people who control management are the same people who implement management's decisions. Thus, there is enough information available so that the community, if it feels alienated by management, can react promptly. Management's zone of maneuverability, a zone within which it can reach decisions without having to constantly justify them or continuously secure agreement to them, is narrow. The magnitude of a zone of maneuverability is highly significant in a turbulent environment. As the environment becomes increasingly turbulent and relatively less predictable, as goals become more comprehensive and diversified, as members of the community have a wider range of interests, professional management's capacity to obtain a common front might be extremely overtaxed under conditions of close scrutiny and direct and potent control by dissenting separatist followers, and management thus might frequently be extremely demoralized.

A relatively larger zone of maneuverability should enable management to design organizational strategies which the dissenting parties will endure. The zone of maneuverability offers a "power pillow" to buffer the aggression of the offended parties that find the strategy not totally satisfying to them at that point in time. In an enterprise, by comparison, management is relatively free. It has more discretion since the controlling group may be absent owners, who become involved only in major policy decisions. Furthermore, it is no secret that management frequently controls its board of directors.

Management in a community, having been given the task to lead, to identify tasks, and to suggest alternatives for their accomplishment, with a limited zone of maneuverability to effectuate those decisions, appears to have a tendency to become either apathetic to the state of the company or to become overzealous in usurping powers from the community. This last strategy is apparently followed in order to accumulate sufficient powers to protect professional management from the all-too-frequent intervention by the community in decisions which are hard to clearly justify, yet are necessary for the company's operations.

The process of rotation which is supposed to protect the community from management's entrenchment in positions and its usurpation of powers, has, however, its negative repercussions: the organization is deprived of continual management, and is thus confronted with frequent policy changes and different leadership styles. While the process of rotation could be a helpful one in a turbulent environment (by avoiding overreliance on one set of policies), it could be disadvantageous if done just for the sake of exercising control. The rotation is an added turbulence beyond that of the environment with which the organization has to cope. Another disadvantage lies in the managerial reward system. Once they are rotated, managers find it difficult to resume positions with less discretion in decision-making or with less responsibility. They go through the "re-entry blues" from a state of hyperactivity to a state wherein they perceive themselves as being pushed to the organizational margins. Thus, rotation might be highly demoralizing, and it probably does not encourage in the best human resources a willingness to undertake managerial positions of hardship when rotation might be the final reward.

Under those conditions, unless professional management is of a different breed, to undertake a managerial function becomes a matter of "social duty," a sacrifice one has to make if the community is to survive. Such a state of affairs does not necessarily bring the best people to these positions.

What, then, are the characteristics, roles, and desired behavior of managers in communities?

THE ROLE OF MANAGEMENT IN SELF-MANAGEMENT

(1) *The Manager as a Leader.* The manager of a community must be self-confident. He should not need for the building of his inner security the power that a managerial position offers. He must feel that he is doing his best and must convince the community of his competence. He needs to be "other oriented" and be interested in the community beyond his self-interest. His major aim in holding the position should be to lead the community toward what he perceives to be an improvement of community affairs. He must be willing to undertake the pressures that leaders experience when the followers do not see instantaneously the benefit of a

proposal. He must be willing to undertake the risk involved in suggesting courses of action in spite of the uncertainty of outcomes, and must be willing to communicate his ideas and convince the community of the prudence of the activity, thereby making his decisions group decisions. This style of leadership must be of the type that instills confidence in the constituents that the manager is not only in control of the situation, but also that he adequately expresses and implements the community's desires and aspirations. If this is not his behavior role and character, a credibility gap might be created, and a strike or other worse disruptions might be the symptomatic reaction of the community.[9]

The manager of a community must have the desire to develop the community as a group, to improve the group dynamics, to lead toward his own obsolescence. This he could do by constantly improving the managerial know-how of the community, and by improving the channels and mechanisms of decision-making so that the community notes effective growth in its capabilities. If this occurs, the community's suspicion that the manager is usurping powers at their expense, or transgressing into their legal domain, will be minimized.

It is doubtful that the manager will ever develop a community to the stage where he will become dispensable; however, there would be self-induced pressure to advance faster ahead in his own development than at the rate of growth of his community. This pressure is the toughest to stimulate and nourish, but it is a necessary condition for successful operation of the community.

Managers with the personality, character, capability and orientation described above are rare since they are a crossbreed of the intellectual and the pragmatist, a staff and line man—leaders in the true sense of the word. Our understanding of what makes people natural or trained leaders is in its infancy, and the scarcity of natural leaders might be one of the bottleneck problems that a community faces.

(2) *The Manager as an Entrepreneur.* Related to the desired characteristics of managers as leaders is the need for them to be entrepreneurs as well. Entrepreneurship will be defined in this context as the willingness to undertake risk via identification and exploitation of opportunities. Leadership as defined above would mean communicating this opportunity and its risks to the community and leading them to identify with the cause and the means suggested.

Entrepreneurship is the willingness to undertake risk. Leadership is the capacity to mobilize followers to a cause, establishing that the followers identify with and accept both the opportunity and the risk the leader identifies with. An entrepreneur is not always a leader. If this is the case, he will be able to identify opportunities and be willing to undertake risk, but he will be incapable of mobilizing the community to accept those risks. If he is entrepreneuring but not leading, the company might be advancing economically, but the community will not necessarily identify with the results and will view management as usurping powers and negating the principle of the community's sovereignty in determining its own destiny. In time of crisis the credibility gap will bring a community confrontation and challenge to management.

In the opposite case, a leader who is not an entrepreneur might mobilize only to conservative, relatively non-risk endeavors. With time, in a changing environment, the community might become economically stagnant; and if the results are failing, there might be another type of confrontation with the members of the organization, and management will be exchanged since it has not produced economic results as desired. Thus, what a community needs (an enterprise needs it as well, but it is not so crucial to its survival) is entrepreneuring leadership.

Securing both leadership and entrepreneurship takes more than hiring the right people with the right personality traits. The organization has to be structured to enable the satisfaction of both leadership and entrepreneurial needs.

The community as structured might satisfy leadership needs, but it apparently does not satisfy the needs of entrepreneurs. Group pressures for conformity do not encourage that individual creativity which is one of the major contributors to entrepreneurial spirit; for at the end of the process, when an action is approved to exploit an opportunity by the group, it may have gone through numerous alterations and criticisms and the entrepreneur might not be able to identify himself with the action anymore. Entrepreneurs must identify with an activity in order to be willing to undertake the risk that the activity calls for. Since the controlling community changes suggested decisions, the end product may be one with which no one individual identifies. If such a process is a prolonged one, people who have entrepreneurial tendencies may plainly "drop out" and try to satisfy their needs outside the system. Such an outcome deprives the community of a very potent driving force necessary for its economic survival.[10]

(3) *The Manager as an Administrator.* In addition to the staffing problem of finding the right people for demanding jobs, there is the problem of allocation of managerial prerogatives. In an enterprise, because there is no legal distinction between policymaking and administration, there is no difficulty in distinguishing the domain of the managerial group from that of the general membership. In a community the total membership is supposed to make decisions of policy content—those decisions that are most crucial to their existence. Management should provide information and leadership in making such decisions, but it is supposed to be unobtrusive and not force issues. Once those policy decisions are made, management is supposed to have the discretion in administrative decisions necessary to implement the policy decisions.

In reality the distinction between policy and administrative decisions is not an easy one to make. There are overlappings, and control over administrative decisions might result in its cumulative form as control over policy decisions. It takes a highly benevolent and enlightened manager to make this distinction workable. In other words, a manager, because of the fact that he is the closest one to the information, can manipulate the timing of information and its character of presentation and thus control policymaking decisions. No legal definition on how decisions should be made, no matter how clearly stated, can assist in making this distinction operative.

Thus, the dysfunctional ambiguity that accompanies the necessary typology between policy decision and administration, which is indispensable for community self-management, accentuates even more the difficulty for management to survive in a community without a nervous breakdown.

(4) *The Manager as a Strategist: Subsystem Integration and Organizational Efficiency.* I have defined a community as an organization whose goals are more than economic. Its goals are comprehensive and include social goals as well. The social goals are not merely means toward economic results as in an enterprise. This distinction is significant since a community pursues social goals for the purpose of achieving them, without necessarily having to rationalize their economic benefits.

In Israel the kibbutz performs a social task by absorbing immigration. It provides the top Israeli military command and political leadership. The kibbutz attempts to achieve goals beyond maximization of economic results, but how much social involvement can or should it afford? Social goals are hard to quantify, and lack of quantification makes justification relatively more difficult. Inability to quantify goals makes the design of congruent strategies a managerial challenge, and the securing of cooperation for such strategies more demanding for leadership.

SUMMARY

(1) *The Importance of Management for Community's Survival.* From the above analyses it should become increasingly clear that management characteristics and behavior are important for the survival of a community. If management, as a group, has no entrepreneurial spirit, no leadership traits, no managerial capacity to design congruent strategies for comprehensive goals, the community will find itself not only with failing economic results but with a social atmosphere too depressing to be endured.

In Yugoslavia, first for ideological reasons and recently for political reasons, management as a group is constantly under attack. The most important factor for making self-management workable is approached in the least positive manner. There are hardly any business schools to train managers; there is hardly any social reward and recognition for their task; they are considered as remnants of capitalism, as a group that is anti-self-management. It is considered to be a radical class that has entrenched itself into undeserved power positions.

The specific role of managers, their training for that purpose, and their reward for adequate action and orientation are of crucial importance for the success of the community. The more we desire self-management, the more enlightened should be our coordinators.

(2) *The Managerial Advantages of a Community.* I have presented above some of the managerial problems of specific importance for the survival of a community in a competitive environment. However, there are some managerial advantages as well: management is capable of implementing change; management has relative freedom to devote time to management as an ongoing activity instead of directing and controlling; and management has relative ease in obtaining information.

When we consider the first advantage, the capacity to implement change, we must recognize that one of the major difficulties of management in an enterprise is to induce and implement change. The fear each individual feels of change and its repercussions leads to entrenchment into one's position and resistance. In Yugoslavia, change is a way of life. Even the Yugoslav communist ideology (1958 Congress of the Communist League) says: "Nothing that has been created must be so sacred for us that it cannot be surpassed and cede its place to what is still more progressive, more free, and more human."

In Yugoslavia, organizations are constantly in the process of adaptation. Salaries are changed, departments removed, new technologies introduced, new labor policies legislated internally, etc. Such rapid change is permitted by an organizational structure that offers economic and psychological security to each individual.[11] Once management presents a decision which involves major change, the whole community gets involved in studying the prudence of the suggestion and its repercussions. In this process management obtains a body of knowledge on the constraints of its initial proposal which in an enterprise usually would take a gathering of consultants and a big budget. Furthermore, once a decision to change is made the necessary alterations and consequent adaptations in the initial proposal are made in the process of implementation, with hardly any management intervention. The community "carries the ball" itself through appointment of committees, through voluntary undertaking of tasks, etc.

It is interesting to note the difference between enterprises and communities as far as organizational change is concerned. In a community it is relatively difficult to induce change. The process of identifying what should change, incorporating various suggestions of the general membership, etc., is a prolonged and, for management, an emotionally exhausting process. However, once the community accepts an idea, swift implementation follows and management is relatively free from the anguish of controlling the implementation. In an enterprise it has been my observation that the opposite phenomenon occurs. Defining what the change should be is relatively a swift process. The difficulty is in implementation, in overcoming the resistance to change.

A manager in a community serves a catalytic function: he assists, guides, and leads the membership toward making certain decisions, and when the decision is made, his role diminishes to that of providing information on the rate of advancement and on the unexpected difficulties encountered. In the ideal state his role is mainly educational.

The second managerial advantage is that of manager as teacher. A manager in a community is more of a teacher and a guide than a policeman. The component of directing and motivating is larger than the component of disciplining and controlling. From self-management stems self-control and self-discipline. For instance, in a Yugoslav factory which I observed in my studies,[12] a young foreman whom I selected at random to observe walked through a plant during his shift. No one rose when he appeared. No one sped up in producing. No one tried to look busy. Some plainly ignored him and continued sitting on benches doing nothing.

When I questioned why they did not work harder when he looked in their direction, he said, "They control themselves. I cannot discipline them. If a worker really loafs, his colleagues will turn him in to the disciplinary committee. Only last week they themselves decided to fire one of the group, since he came once too late to work." Since the group shares the results of its work, anyone who does not contribute as expected affects the income of others. The system itself, then, induces group self-discipline and control, which should free management to deal with strategy formulation for the community to approve, with securing maximum support for courses of action to be selected, with motivation in general and the processes of democratic decision-making. In other words, management has to exercise most of the true leadership and entrepreneurship, rather than to administer the implementation. This should lead to effective operation and accelerated personal and organizational growth.

Third, but not least important, the system fosters openness. Since all workers participate, there is little opportunity for an individual to monopolize and bias information. Open and sincere discussions take place, and management is offered insights into the repercussions of the decisions it suggests before they are implemented. This saves management the expenses and uncalled-for aggravations which are usually generated by difficulties which surface after a decision is made and which could have been anticipated if people were more open and willing to present their information, rather than monopolize it as a source of power. A manager as a leader, a teacher who witnesses the personal growth of the members of the community, gets a unique satisfaction in a community. He gets a genuine opportunity to satisfy leadership needs, to identify what the organization needs and what the followers want, and then design a strategy that can mobilize the community and at the same time forward it economically. Although this opportunity exists in enterprises as well, the need for leadership traits is neither so pronounced nor so crucial as in a community.

The Relevance of Community Management in the United States—a Speculation

The increased complexity of the postindustrial society, moving from an atomistic to a fish-scale environment, is generating conflicts that must be resolved. These pressures, present in both totalitarian and free societies, have increased the power of government and endanger democracy. The self-management system, based on the community organizational structure, appears to offer a new approach to this problem, an approach that includes a decentralized, participative, polyvalent mechanism of conflict resolution.

I thus believe that the classical enterprise as defined above is in decline in the United States. Labor is increasingly considered as an asset to be enriched rather than as a production input to be consumed and discarded once no longer needed.

Goals of enterprises are becoming more comprehensive in nature and are not geared exclusively toward higher economic efficiency. We are now talking about optimum GNP, rather than maximum GNP. We are turning toward the social relations in the society. Labor is getting an increasing share of managerial prerogatives by being a constraint in what management can decide. Thus, the veto power of labor is a potent source of power, and they might share in managing the company if they are put on Boards of Directors. As the economic dimension of the environment becomes more affluent, as people turn toward social goals and the satisfaction of individual psychological needs, they will turn for fulfillment to the organizations where they spend most of their waking time. With this change, relationships among people, social climate, and patterns of subordination will change and pressure on the managerial group will be to encourage the emergence of the enlightened management as described above for communities.

I wish to state that I believe that the changes will never be of the magnitude capable of changing the patterns and concepts of ownership, such as the communists tend to believe about the future of the capitalist system. This will not occur, I believe, because there is no need to change ownership in order to obtain managerial prerogatives. The sharing of managerial prerogatives is the crucial variable in securing labor's commitments to an organization—a wish capitalists have, no less than communists.

I believe that these changes in the environment and in the character of future organizations, with the organization becoming more of a community than an enterprise, pose unique and demanding pressures on management, more than on any other group, to reorient its views, its style, and its ability to operate under new reward mechanisms.

Thus, the role of executive education and of research in this field cannot be understated if communities are to develop without the accompanying problems that have surfaced elsewhere.

NOTES

1. Mezzo level analysis refers to the organizational unit. Micro analysis focuses on individuals in organizations or on other inputs into the production process.
2. It might be interesting to note that in the capitalist system the contributors of capital are considered "insiders" to the organization as far as the prerogatives of management are concerned. Labor on the other hand, although they are "inside" the organization, are considered "outsiders." Thus management represents capital, while labor has to use outside sources of power as pressure groups to express its interests. Furthermore, labor was not considered as worthy of managerial prerogatives since it was transient. Capital appeared to be the permanent component that was taking the risk in the company. The reality in modern economy appears to be different. I suggest that labor is less mobile than capital. It is the stockholder that is transient while labor, once investing its time in one company, will be less prone to move around.
3. For a detailed comparison and elaboration of the subject, see I. Adizes and F.J. Weston, "Comparative Models of Social Responsibility," *Journal of the Academy of Management*, Vol. II, no. 1, March 1973.
4. In my opinion, the Yugoslav self-management system makes the same conceptual mistake by giving only to labor the managerial prerogatives (precluding capital), just as in capitalist systems, capital precludes labor. I believe, as I said above, that all inputs should have equal representation. For supporting evidence and reasoning, see my article "Economic Change in Yugoslavia," *East Europe*, 21, no. 10, October 1972.
5. In this paper "decision-making" is equivalent to "choice-making," i.e., selecting the course of action. It does not include the whole process of arriving at the various alternatives for this choice-making.

6. For more on this subject, see my book, Chapter 6, on labor relations: Ichak Adizes, *Industrial Democracy—Yugoslav Style* (New York: Free Press, 1971).
7. For a description of an actual strike I have observed in Yugoslavia and recorded, see ibid.
8. For more on this subject, see ibid., Chapter 8.
9. Ibid, Chapter 6.
10. For further in-depth discussion on this topic, see ibid, Chapter 8.
11. For recording of actual discussions and processes of change, see my book, ibid., Chapters 4-5.
12. Ibid., Chapters 4-5.

2

THE INTEGRATION OF LABOR AND SOCIAL CAPITAL UNDER WORKERS' CONTROL

by Edward Kardelj
Member, Council of Federation,
Yugoslavia

DURING the first years following the victory of the socialist revolution in Yugoslavia, the concept of social property was held to be identical with that of state property, both from the legal point of view and with regard to the management of social resources. The only way for revolution to change social relations was to nationalize the means of production, expropriate the capitalist owners, turn private capital into state property, and consolidate this new state property through adequate centralization. Most countries on the road to socialism, especially economically underdeveloped ones, still go through a longer or shorter phase of state-property relations, and are likely to do so in the future.

Even during the first years of socialist construction in Yugoslavia, however, the state character of social property bore the seeds of basic social contradictions. These reflected themselves in the separation of the workers and their labor from the direct management of social capital[1] and resulted in the alienation of "surplus-value" which gradually fell under the control of a bureaucracy or technocracy. It became evident, not only in Yugoslavia but also in other socialist countries, that under the centralization of social capital, its management and control tended to be exercised in such a way that the workers were excluded from even the ordinary democratic supervision of the use of social resources. In Yugoslavia it was soon recognized that this contradiction posed a socio-economic and political problem. The attempt to overcome this problem generated the idea and practice of socialist self-management in Yugoslavia. Thus self-management emerged as a natural reaction to the tendency of identifying social property with bureaucratic and technocratic monopoly exercised by the state and its economic apparatus. In other words, self-management

39

was an attempt to prevent bureaucratic, technocratic and anti-democratic deformations in the development of socialist relations.

The socio-historical significance of socialist self-management is that it creates forms of production-relations which are based on social property and in which appropriation is based only on labor. The worker appropriates *directly* on the basis of his work, freed from all forms of wage-labor relations between himself and the owner of capital, i.e., the state which acts as a collective owner of capital. The worker, however, does not do this autarchically, anarchically or as an owner in his own right, but in interdependence with, and fully responsible to, the equal rights of his fellow workers. By this fact alone social property ceases to express a relationship between the workers and the state. It articulates instead the relationship among the working people themselves.

In conditions of socialist self-management, social-property relations cannot be expressed in terms of classical legal formulae, but only in terms of an essentially new system of economic and political relations, based on the rights and mutual responsibilities of the workers. The social means of production belong to all those who work. This is the most important objective condition for their labor and for their freedom as workers and creators. But no one can have private property title to these means of production. In this sense social property is "everybody's" and "nobody's." At the same time, however, the social means of production are the workers personal tool and thus the means with which they earn their personal incomes. Thus social property is both the common class property of all the workers and a form of individual property of those who work. Social-property relations therefore are no longer relations between "owners" and "non-owners"—which, practically, means relations between buyers and sellers of labor-power or between the state and the workers. They are relations among the workers themselves who *jointly* control the means of production and *individually* appropriate the product of their labor, who place their *common means of production* into the service of the *individual creative power and ability of workers* for the purpose of achieving the best possible *common and individual* results. This contradictory nature of social property should necessarily find expression in the system of production and economic relations in associated labor based on self-management, as well as in the political order and the legal institutions which should ensure this system.

The structure of these socio-economic relations in the Yugoslav system of self-management was initiated by the Federal Constitution of 1963. It was further developed by the economic reform of 1965. But even now the process has not gone beyond its incipient stage. This has resulted in an aggravation of the contradictions between the relations created by the introduction and development of self-management in the work organizations[2] on the one hand, and on the other, relations resulting from the remaining forms of statist and technocratic-monopolistic appropriation of "surplus-labor" in re-investment and the circulation of social capital. This contradiction has in fact become a serious obstacle to the further development of socialist self-management and a threat to the unity and stability of the economic system. The continued existence and further aggravation of this contradiction might engender new social differentiations and political conflict. To some extent it has already done so.

There are only two ways of overcoming this contradiction. The first of these does not offer a genuine and lasting solution. It would consist in a return to the centralization of social capital in the hands of the Federal Government or in the Governments of the constituent Republics. Such centralization could only be based on state coercion. This is the alternative offered by the ideology and practice of technocracy, bureaucracy, and statist centralism.

The other alternative consists in a resolute effort to ensure the integration of labor and social capital under workers' control. This, in fact, was and still is the real aim of the social and economic reform started in Yugoslavia in 1965.[3]

The constitutional amendments adopted in 1971[4] facilitated and have accelerated the realization of this second alternative. In a somewhat over-simplified and schematic way, the principle underlying these amendments can be summed up as follows. From the total income of associated labor and from the total income of individual basic organizations of associated labor, certain deductions have to be made.[5] These include social cost, reserves, and similar social funds. These deductions are made either on the basis of self-management agreements and social compacts,[6] or on the basis of workers' constitutional rights or of decisions by the socio-political communities[7] based on these rights. The rest of the income is managed and disposed of by the workers in the basic organizations of associated labor. Through these basic organizations the workers, in their common interest, pool their labor and income in work organizations, integrated systems, banks, institutions of wholesale trade, foreign trade, etc. They retain, however, their right to exercise economic and political control over the use of "their" part of the mass of associated resources. This means that these resources can be spent only in agreement with the workers in the basic organizations of associated labor, or only on the basis of the terms of their self-management agreements. A basic organization of associated labor has the right to participate in the distribution of jointly earned income in proportion to the contribution made to the generation of this income by its workers with their "living," i.e., current labor and through their management of the social means of production, i.e., in proportion to their contribution to the successful development of their organization of associated labor made with their own creative work. Since these means of production are the result of both the past labor[8] of the workers in this particular organization and of the past labor of the workers in other organizations of associated labor, they are neither the private nor the group property of the workers. They are social property, i.e., the common property of all workers in associated labor.

This system, based on the equal rights and obligations of all workers participating in associated labor, guarantees that no "state-run" or any other economic organization in which social capital is concentrated or which engages in financial transactions, can use "its" capital in a monopolistic way. Any such organization must bear full economic and political responsibility to the workers in each basic organization of associated labor, and, through them, to each worker individually for his share in the social capital it works with or manages. This system should ensure that, in principle, each dinar of the workers' "surplus-labor" or "past" labor that enters into the circulation of social capital should remain under their own management. That is, that dinar should return to them or be spent under their control.

It is only under such conditions that workers have real economic and political power over the economic and social functions of social property which they can subordinate to their class, working, social and cultural interests. In this way the *income* of a basic work organization becomes the *beginning* of the socialization and circulation of social "surplus-labor" which insures expanded reproduction and social reproduction. This income is at the same time also the *end* of this process because the results of this productivity of social labor—except the part accruing to socially constituted welfare and government expenditure funds—*are returned* to the income of work collectives and individual workers. Thus the *contribution* made by a collective with its total "living" and "past" labor to the rise in economic productivity of the total social labor has a twofold function: it becomes a title to income generated by total social labor, and also the principal yardstick for measuring participation in its distribution. It becomes a criterion for the distribution of personal income according to work done.

Under such conditions "surplus-labor" becomes part of the workers' "necessary labor" because the economic function of social capital becomes a direct function of the associated labor of all workers, and the "surplus-value" in the class antagonistic sense of this term, tends to disappear. It is no longer alienated from the worker but is part of the income which he himself controls on a self-management basis.

Only this system of economic relations, rights, and obligations, based on the Constitution and on law, can ensure a relatively free development of our socialist society in which workers, as the principal managers of the economy, will subordinate to their current and long-term interests all centers of the professional management of labor and income. Of course this does not imply any lessening of the responsibility of the professional management nor of the need for capable professional managers. But the managerial centers in the economy must be kept separate from the political power apparatus, i.e., the state. They must be tied instead even more directly to the self-managing basis of associated labor. They must become part of it, instead of exercising economic power over the workers and their income.

By controlling their income, workers should also be enabled to exercise a decisive influence on the development and on the activities of various public services which are still to a greater or lesser extent managed by the state. That is, self-management should gradually extend to public health, education, social welfare, child care, etc.

In recent discussions, especially in connection with the implementation of the constitutional amendments of 1971, we have heard the view that work organizations should not earn any income on the basis of management of "past" labor, i.e., on the basis of the investment of part of their income in other work organizations or what is referred to as joint ventures. This view is substantiated by the assertion that "past" labor, i.e., capital, does not produce any new value, so that any income earned on its account would mean exploitation of other workers. The essence of the matter however does not lie in the truism that the "past," materialized labor, i.e., capital, does not by itself create any new value since new value can only be created by workers with their "living," current productive labor. What is essential here is what happens to "past" labor while it still exists as a value materialized and accumulated in the form of social capital, i.e., while it has not yet been expended. The real question is by whom and in what way it is appropriated, who manages it, and in what way those who manage it relate to those who generate it and to the workers organized on a self-management basis.

Marx pointed out that "surplus-labor" or "surplus-value" created by "living labor" is partly appropriated as profit by the capitalist owner of the means of production, and partly as the profit or interest of banks or other representatives of financial capital, or as the ground rent of land-owners, or in other forms characteristic of the distribution of profits in the capitalist mode of production. Precisely for this reason Marx emphasized that the capitalist system of production could not be understood if these relations were not considered in the light of the unity of the production process and the circulation of capital in which a large part of the "surplus-value" created by "living," productive labor is generated.

Marx pointed out that "surplus-labor" or "surplus-value" created by "living labor" is partly appropriated as profit by the capitalist owner of the means of production, and partly as the profit or interest of banks or other representatives of financial capital, or as the ground rent of land-owners, or in other forms characteristic of the distribution of profits in the capitalist mode of production. Precisely for this reason Marx emphasized that the capitalist system of production could not be understood if these relations were not considered in the light of the unity of the production process and the circulation of capital in which a large part of the "surplus-value" created by "living," productive labor is generated.

The question arises: Are there, under socialism, no elements of economic relations and no problems of this kind at all?

Research in Yugoslavia has shown not only that such elements do exist but also that they are the source of one of the basic contradictions in our society. It is true that in Yugoslavia the categories "capital," "surplus-labor," surplus-value," etc., are losing their class-antagonistic character to the extent to which all means of production are becoming the common property of all those who work. However, what we wish to point out here is that in Yugoslavia, as for that matter in all other socialist countries, a form of the alienation of the means of production from the workers still exists in the surviving aspects of state-property relations and technocratic-managerial monopoly. And this applies in particular to the sphere of management of accumulated "past" labor, or social capital. So it is not maintained that some new value is being created in this sphere, but only that a considerable part of the value generated by the workers is taken away from them.

According to one view, the workers cannot possibly control on a self-management basis the results of accumulated "past" labor, i.e., the means of expanded production, simply because these means do not consist only of their own "surplus" or "past" labor but of the "past" labor of all workers in associated labor. Therefore they should be managed by some other social agent, not by the workers themselves. This is another way of saying that socialism can only exist when social capital is monopolistically managed and unrestrictedly disposed of by the state apparatus or a small segment of bureaucracy and technocracy, entrenched either in the so-called political sphere or in business organizations—it does not matter which—and always relying on the political power of the state.

Such assertions not only turn all logic upside down, but they are an obvious expression of the ideology of statism and bureaucratic-technocratic monopoly.

Why should a socialist society be alien to the idea that workers, collectively organized in their organizations of associated labor with their organs of self-management, are able to manage social capital with at least as much responsibility to society and the other workers as some bureaucratic-technocratic organs alienated from labor and production and oriented exclusively or predominantly toward the political leadership of the state and its apparatus, organs which may easily turn insensitive to the authentic interests of the workingman? Why should a socialist society be alien to the idea that associated workers directly in charge of the management of social capital would be just as interested in having the most capable and successful scientific, technical, and business apparatus as is the state or any general board or similar center of economic or political power? Why, finally, should a socialist society be alien to the idea that the responsibilities of work collectives in the management of income which is not theirs alone, but is also common to all, could be as clearly defined and precisely formulated in the Constitution and the laws as are the responsibilities of the state apparatus or the managing bodies of banks and the like?

The ideologists of statism and of bureaucratic-technocratic monopoly do not even want to hear such questions. Just as private ownership is, for the capitalist, a sacred cow that may not be talked about, let alone touched, so the ideology of bureaucracy and technocracy sees in technocratic-bureaucratic monopoly on social capital the quintessence of socialism or "the end of history."

I do not by any means wish to idealize the system of workers' self-management or, in particular, this system of income distribution. Under conditions of commodity production it will undoubtedly always be under pressure. There will always be tendencies to take advantage of and profit unilaterally from the common income or social capital. Man's nature cannot be changed over-night by a mere change in the system. Not even the working class's feeling of solidarity can suppress the selfish wish to live, if possible, at some one else's expense. But there is one thing that can be asserted with certainty: it is easier to counteract such tendencies in a self-management system, either through the self-managers themselves, or through the democratic mechanisms of society, than it is under the conditions of bureaucratic-technocratic domination of the working class.

Criticism of bureaucratic-technocratic tendencies should obviously not be directed against the technical and other kinds of intelligentsia in general or against the people holding managerial functions in work organizations. The overwhelming majority of white collar workers in Yugoslavia are as conscious and as closely linked to the self-management system as the physical workers.

Technocratic-managerial monopoly cannot survive as an independent factor in production relations. Either it will degenerate in the direction of a private-property-based capitalist monopoly—which is not a realistic possibility in a socialist society—or it will merge with the state and its apparatus. In other words, it will become an instrument to restore state-property relations in production. It is this second alternative that could become reality in Yugoslavia if associated labor and the forces of revolution should lack the strength and ability to subordinate the functions of management and of the disposal of the social means of production to the interests of and control by free workers in freely associated labor based on self-management.

The integration of labor and social capital in the form of income of basic organizations of associated labor does not lead to the "atomization" of social capital under monopolistic management by workers. It is an undisputable fact that in Yugoslav society, as in all other modern societies, the concentration of the means of production and a corresponding centralization of social capital are a necessity. This necessity is not only imposed by modern technological development but also by the socialist system of economic planning. Thus the problem does not lie in the concentration of the means of production and in the centralization of social capital, nor for that matter in social planning on various levels of associated labor. Everything depends on the way these processes are realized and on the way they influence socioeconomic relations in a socialist society. Workers will support this kind of centralization of social capital to the extent to which they will see in it a means of asserting their own working and creative efforts, and to the extent to which the struggle for higher productivity of social labor, and their own contributions to it, will be conducive to improvement in the material, social, and cultural conditions of the work and life. If they are not maximally interested in this problem today, it is because of certain inadequacies in the system as it is operating at this time. The way to overcome these is to clarify relations between "past" and "living" labor, between workers and their accumulated "surplus-labor" and, I would add, to define those institutional forms which will clearly determine the nature of all these relations and mutual responsibilities among working people in associated labor.

The concrete form and content of these economic relations will be partly regulated by legislation and partly by self-management agreements, and the by-laws of, and contracts made by, organizations of associated labor. These legal acts should spell out the way in which workers and their organizations will exercise control over their joint income or participate in its management, including the distribution of income earned by associated labor and by joint investment of income.

This will not only counter the fragmentation and "isolation" of work organizations, it will also strengthen the link between the interests of the workers and their mutual economic and social relationships. It is for this reason that both the economic and social solidarity of the working people must become an essential part of self-management economic relations based on the social ownership of the means of production.

This does not mean that in our system there is no place for common funds in which resources are invested without reimbursement, or for the allocation of resources for the purpose of preventing economic disturbances, adjusting economic trends, ensuring financial reserves, providing economic assistance to the underdeveloped parts of the country, etc. But decisions on such allocations without reimbursement can be made in only two ways: either on the basis of voluntary self-management agreements among work organizations concluded for a specific period of time and based on their bylaws, or on the basis of statute in cases provided for by the Constitution. However, these funds should be strictly confined to their purpose and should not be turned into a kind of state capital.

The recognition of the above-mentioned economic and political rights and responsibilities of the workers regarding the control of "past" labor does not mean that the state can or should lose the right and possibility by means of economic policy to influence the adjustment of relations in the sphere of integration of labor and capital in order to ensure economic stability and safeguard the equality of the workers. On the contrary, at the present level of economic development, the self-management system cannot, by itself, and without reliance on the state, resolve all contradictions within the economic processes.

The withering away of the state can only be said to have begun on a major scale when workers associated on the basis of self-management begin to manage common social capital directly from their work place, not through some kind of political representatives—except to the extent to which the state's regulative and planning role is indispensable.

The historical meaning of social property under conditions of socialist self-management is that it overcomes the alienation of labor from social capital. For social property brings about the integration of labor and social capital. This integration cannot be achieved through any form of property monopoly on capital which, under capitalism, leads to the appropriation of "surplus-labor" by capital, and under socialism manifests itself in the residual form of the state-property right to social capital and the subordination of labor and the workers to this right. *The integration of labor and social capital can only be achieved by workers exercising direct control over the objective material conditions of their labor, that is, through the socioeconomic unification of "living" and "past" labor materialized in the means of production and in social capital in general.*

NOTES

1.   Throughout this text the term *social capital* is used to denote the part of income of
     associated labor which, in a socialist society, is accumulated and socialized as the
     working people's common means of expanded reproduction. The term only relates to
     the *economic functions* of capital as the sum total of the social means of reproduction,

not to capital as a property or as a *class force* which reproduces capital property relations.

2. "Work organization"*(radna organizacija)* is the general term for organizations of associated labor under the system of self-management, both in the economic and the legal sense. Work organizations are either enterprises engaged in production and commerce or institutions concerned with non-economic activities (health, education, science, etc.).

    A "basic organization of associated labor" *(osnovna organizacija udruzenoq rada)* is a part of a work organization which constitutes an economic-technological entity the results of whose work (products or services) can be expressed in terms of market value. According to the Constitution and the autonomous bylaw working people in the basic organizations of associated labor regulate directly and, as equals, their mutual economic and other relations, manage social resources entrusted to them, decide on the distribution of income earned, etc.

3. On June 30, 1971, the Federal Assembly passed 23 amendments (XX to XLII) to the Federal Constitution of 1963. In addition to the principles concerning socioeconomic principal aims of the reform were, and still are, adequate reform of the price system, the determination of a realistic rate of exchange of the national currency in international trade, etc.; a transition from extensive to intensive methods of business, i.e., the creation of conditions for a faster rise in labor productivity, a more rational division of labor; modernization of the economy, cooperation, integration, greater participation in the international division of labor, and improvement in the living conditions of working people. All this was to be aided by a more marked and consistent switch to economic and market criteria in business. At the same time, the reform introduced significant changes in the use and control of social resources in work organizations on the basis of the principles of self-management.

4. On June 30, 1971 the Federal Assembly passed 23 amendments (XX to XLII) to the Federal Constitution of 1963. In addition to the principles concerning socio-economic relations, the amendments also introduced significant reforms in the political structure of the country. The functions and competences of the Federation have been greatly curtailed and confined to foreign policy, national defense, the unity of the market, and the fundamentals of the socioeconomic and political system, while all other matters have been left to the jurisdiction of the constituent Republics and Autonomous Provinces. The amendments also introduce changes in the structure of the federal agencies, the most significant among which is the formation of the Presidency of the Socialist Federal Republic of Yugoslavia as a collective "head of state."

5. The switch to market forms of business and self-financing of the economy was initiated already in 1958. Until that time the economy was predominantly financed from state investment funds and the budget. Now, furthermore, the state was no longer competent to fix workers' wages and salaries, nor the rate of capital accumulation of enterprises which had begun to finance their operations from their own income realized on the market.

    According to the new system, income is formed in the following way: from the revenue grossed by a work organization (or a basic organization of associated labor) from the sale of its products or services on the market, material costs and depreciation must first be deducted; what is left constitutes the income of the workers of this organization. Part of this income is used for the workers' personal consumption (personal incomes), another for expanded reproduction (accumulation), and the rest for the satisfaction of the general social and common needs of the working people (education, health, social security, national defense, state administration, etc.).

6. Self-management agreements *(samoupravni sporazumi)* and social compacts *(drusvtveni dogovori)* were introduced, as a new constitutional category, by the constitutional amendments of 1971. Through them, a large number of economic and social questions can now be regulated by direct agreement among working people themselves or with the participation of social bodies and agencies, rather than by legislation.

    Self-management agreements are concluded by the basic organizations of associated labor, work organizations, etc., to regulate their association, to determine their mutual economic and other relations with regard to the distribution of enterprise income and personal income, joint capital investment, etc., and to lay down criteria for the adjustment of their interests to broader common interests. A self-management agreement is binding on all organizations of associated labor which have concluded it or have subsequently acceded to it.

Social compacts are concluded among organizations of associated labor and their chambers of economy, sociopolitical communities, and trade unions with a view to adjusting and regulating economic and development policies, the basic criteria for the distribution of enterprise and personal incomes, etc. A social compact is binding on all organizations and communities which have signed it.

3

FURTHER DEVELOPMENT OF SELF-MANAGEMENT IN YUGOSLAVIA AND ITS SOCIOPOLITICAL ASPECTS

by Anton Vratusa
Deputy Prime Minister,
Yugoslavia

THE adoption of the law on Workers' Self-Management in economic enterprises laid the cornerstone for the system of self-management in Yugoslavia. By this act, the idea of the emancipation of labor began to be translated into a fact of life. Looking back over twenty years of implementation of workers' self-management, we should now be able to draw some general conclusions about its significance, achievements, and further prospects.

When the system was introduced in 1950, it was limited to economic enterprises. Soon, however, it was extended to all types of organizations.

The commune, as the basic sociopolitical community, was built on this new foundation, and it is from the self-governing commune that the whole new social and political structure of Yugoslavia rises. The period of "administrative socialism," which immediately after the revolution had concentrated all power in the hands of the State, was over, giving way to new democratic relationships. The Constitutional Law of 1953, the Constitution of 1963, the Socio-Economic Reform of 1965, and especially, the Constitutional Amendments of 1968-1971, are landmarks in the Yugoslav socialist experience.

Decentralization is not an end in itself. However, decentralization is the foundation, the building block, of self-management. From the very beginning, the unity of the Yugoslav peoples has been a precondition for the creation of a socialist self-governing community in which all peoples will be assured of full emancipation and self-assertion as well as cooperation and solidarity, including the extension of assistance to less developed republics and areas. The decentralization of the economy and of the sociopolitical structure as a whole went hand in hand with a process of democratic integration within the framework of self-government. This integration is made imperative by the pursuit of the interests of all the working people.

The League of Communists of Yugoslavia initiated these processes ideologically and politically, and at the same time it adapted its own organizational structure and working methods to the new conditions.

THE ROLE OF THE LEAGUE OF COMMUNISTS

There are two erroneous interpretations of the League's role in this development which should be refuted from the outset.

The first interpretation is one often held abroad. Under pressure from below, it is said, the League of Communists tried to adapt itself to the new realities by initiating the process of its own democratization, divesting itself of state power and retaining only its ideological role in society.

The other interpretation is the product of a "liberal humanistic" way of thinking. It holds that the League of Communists had discharged its revolutionary function since it was no longer required during this stage of "evolution."

Both these interpretations are not supported by the facts. They negate the historic role of the League of Communists in the evolution of self-management. Through its political and ideological action, the League of Communists has been the vanguard force in the overall democratic transformation. If the League of Communists ceased to play this role, further socialist and democratic evolution would be unimaginable either in theory or in practice.

The further democratization of society assumes the further democratization of the League of Communists itself. So far, the League has been the initiator of all activities designed to sustain the democratic transformation of Yugoslav society and all its institutions, in line with self-management. In the process, the League has developed and democratized itself.

CURRENT LEGISLATION

The series of current constitutional reforms on the basis of self-management in Yugoslavia should ensure that it is the workers themselves who make the decisions regarding the results of their work, including their surplus product. These reforms should enhance social relationships and the creation of mechanisms for resolving social conflicts, not only within the working organizations but within the sociopolitical communities in general. They should counteract any tendencies on the part of sociopolitical communities to closet themselves off against one another, or to disintegrate the integral market. The reforms should help the constituent nations and nationalities of Yugoslavia to overcome contradictions in their mutual relations through democratic procedures, democratically recon-

ciling conflicting interests within the working class and the working
people as a whole.

Upon the resolution of these problems depends not only the socioeconomic stability of the workers' position, but also the unity of the socioeconomic system and the strength of the entire Yugoslav community.

In socioeconomic terms, the primary goal of the recently introduced
constitutional reforms was the extension of the workers'control over the
surplus value of their labor which had been slipping out from under them,
tending to concentrate in the banks, the head offices of large integrated
enterprises, and in various public funds and institutions alienated from
direct workers' control. The workers' share in the returns from income
earned from the operation of economic units and from the general increase of the GNP posed other problems.

Thus, while the essential task in the early sixties was to ensure that
workers and their collectives disposed of freely the income earned from
direct market transactions, the problem today is how to relate the worker's
income to the increased social productivity in proportion to his own contribution to this increase, especially trying to prevent any private individual or managerial group from gaining control over this process.

All this is supposed to be regulated by the Constitution, especially in
the amendments of 1971, and implemented by democratic consensus and
agreement among the various republics, autonomous provinces, and
organizations of associated labor. The integration of labor and social
capital is a basic condition for self-management, as the basic socioeconomic relationship in the country.

In sociopolitical terms, the basic problems today are: (1) how to ensure the democratic functioning of self-management as a basis of the
whole sociopolitical system; (2) how to develop efficiency in the system
based on personal responsibility in the production process and on all levels
of public activity; (3) how to prevent organizations from isolating themselves from progressive trends in society in general, and from escaping
general social control; and (4) how to ensure the influence of associated
labor on decision-making in public affairs at every level. Solving these
problems will involve the following tasks: (1) to complete the action against
the state monopoly (bureaucracy), the action which started with the introduction of self-management; (2) to fight the managerial technocratia,
which, in the pretended name of efficiency, is increasing its power and
alienating labor; and (3) to struggle against interference of noneconomic
factors in self-management.

These are indeed complex tasks. Their fulfiilment not only requires
perception of the true interests of all concerned and the creation of
adequate mechanisms of self-management from the working and local
communities to the communal assembly, but also requires continuous
political and ideological activity. Only under such conditions can the commune become the basic sociopolitical community and the cornerstone of
the entire sociopolitical system, within which the assembly system, an integral part of self-management, provides the forum for the democratic
resolution of conflicting interests.

SELF-MANAGEMENT AND THE GOVERNMENTAL MACHINERY

During the last few years the structure, organization, and working methods of the Yugoslav parliamentary system have undergone certain changes. It is evident that maximum changes and adjustments are necessary in order to increase the role of the workers and of the commune in the decision-making processes of the Assembly. The whole assembly system must divest itself of processes and influences pervading the assemblies or parliaments in multiparty political systems, characterized as they are by the struggle for power. In such instances there is little room for the direct influence of the "grass roots."

In order to guarantee the continuous renewal of assembly membership and the deprofessionalization of political office, i.e., to increase the "grass roots" support, the principle of rotation and of limited re-election rights was introduced in the Constitution of 1963. Limitations were placed upon the right of the voters to reelect to office a person who had already served a term in that same office, despite the fact that he might enjoy their full confidence. This was the price the community had to pay if it wanted to keep its representative bodies continually open and thus less liable to develop the ills of bureaucratization, and if it wanted to make participation in public affairs widely accessible to the working people. It was believed that these principles would enhance political disalienation in a very concrete way and would offer an efficient instrument for overcoming the domination of one person over another.

Experience demonstrated that these measures did not suffice to ensure the transformation of the entire assembly system. Good as it may have been in theory, the principle of rotation, involving the election of half of the assembly members every second year within the four-year term of that body, had to be abandoned for practical considerations, and the regulations limiting reelection had to be relaxed. Instead, it became apparent that a more profound reform of the electoral system itself was necessary to make the assemblies, in structure and membership, more responsive and more closely linked to the interests of workers and of the self-managing organizational units of society in general.

APPLYING SELF-MANAGEMENT TO INTERNATIONAL RELATIONS IN YUGOSLAVIA

The equality of the nations and the nationalities of Yugoslavia was stipulated by the Constitution of 1963. The implementation of this principle, however, does not depend upon the Constitution alone. It depends upon all the people. Problems of equality among nations and nationalities cannot be solved by separatist pressures nor by chauvinist unitarianism or demagoguery. They must be solved democratically, taking into account both specific and general interests. Priorities have to be set, and the means must be adequate to the goals. During the time of what we call administrative socialism, methods and forms of organization were different from those that are appropriate today, now that self-government has been established. But the basic premise is the same: contradictions and antagonisms cannot be whisked away or bypassed. They have to be solved.

Yugoslavia today is again faced with a number of unsolved questions, not only in the economic sphere but also in the sociopolitical structure. There is no doubt that these questions can be solved positively only through the further strengthening of self-management and the adaptation of the entire sociopolitical system to it.

This means that self-management should transcend the limits of the factory or enterprise and become the basic principle of all socioeconomic relations and of the whole political system of the country. It provides an appropriate formula to counteract still present tendencies toward reinstating various types of private ownership, bureaucracy, autarchy within the limits of narrow-minded nationalism—both in the guise of great-nation nationalism and of the separatism of the republics.

The Constitutional Amendments of 1971 cut radically into the roots of great-nation hegemony and eliminated whatever obstacles that may have remained to block the self-assertion of every nation and nationality in Yugoslavia. They clearly defined and strengthened the autonomy of the constituent republics, and democratized the relations among them. The second phase of the constitutional reform, now in operation, will complete the process of restructuring the whole political system in the country. Focusing on the basic working organizations and local sociopolitical communities, it will reform the assembly system from bottom to top in such a way that the assemblies will really represent these basic units throughout the whole sociopolitical system.

DIRECT DEMOCRACY INSTEAD OF PARLIAMENTARY REPRESENTATION

The self-managing economic rights of the worker (self-determination; equality, based on the distribution of income in accordance with on-the-job performance; participation in the management of funds for the expansion of social production) are the foundation of his political rights as a citizen. This means the worker, at his place of work, must have the possibility to act effectively on the development of the political system needed to ensure the expansion of his influence on all spheres of social life.

This implies a transformation of the representative political system of indirect classical parliamentary democracy into a system of direct socialist democracy. The traditional political party system is the basis of a representative parliamentary system in which the citizen is represented by a general representative elected for a given term. It necessarily becomes an instrument in the struggle for power and a source of political demagoguery, no matter whether it is based on one or a number of political parties. It alienates the citizen and generates within him a dichotomy between worker and citizen. The aim is to eliminate this dichotomy, and it is possible only through decisive participation and direct involvement of the working person from his own work place, through his competent delegate who works with him and lives in the same community.

The positive contribution of the classical parliamentary system to the development of bourgeois democracy and democracy in general cannot be denied. This does not mean, however, that the party system represents the pinnacle of political democracy. After all, even its most fervent advocates admit that not only the parliamentary system, but the entire order based upon it, is in deep crisis today.

A sociopolitical system based on self-management is being designed to overcome the dichotomy between worker and citizen, i.e., between those who produce and those who make the decision on disposition of the results of that labor.

Both in the organizations of associated labor and in the organs of state power, the workers' role is problem oriented and not based on political affiliation, no matter whether he acts directly or through different forms by his elected delegates. A genuine delegate of associated labor cannot be a representative of a general type. He must be a delegate competent to deal with the problems under consideration and must enjoy the trust of associated labor. Thus, the assembly system in Yugoslavia cannot be developed as a house of representatives in the classical sense. The Yugoslav assembly is supposed to be a body where delegates of associated labor make decisions on those questions for which they have been delegated to find solutions, this delegation being both on the basis of the general confidence they enjoy and on their competence to cope with the actual problems involved.

It should be added that the principle of solidarity among the working people plays an important role in the socioeconomic and political relationships of self-management. As a matter of fact, it is a specific kind of barometer measuring the degree to which relationships of self-management have become a reality. In a system of statist bureaucratic management, there is not much room for workers' solidarity nor for any other manifestation of initiative. In a centrally planned system, everything has been "planned in advance," "foreseen," etc., whereas self-management orients person to person. It makes it incumbent upon every worker to look for comrades in the process of production, to achieve solidarity and social consensus. Self-management is based on moral and material commitments rather than upon legal sanctions. This does not mean that it can exist outside the structure of state organs and law. State organs and law, including sanctions, will continue to exist, but their function is to safeguard the free development of self-management and to ensure, within the limits provided for by law, that everybody respects the rights of others and fulfills their own commitments.

To pit state organs against organs of self-management, to brand as antagonistic to self-management the protective or administrative measures undertaken by state agencies under the control and on behalf of the working class, is as erroneous as to insist on the dichotomy between worker and citizen or economics and politics, which the self-management system is designed to overcome.

If decision-making power in the assembly system belongs to the workers, organized on the basis of self-management and if the responsible social bodies in the commune, the republic, and the federation are obliged in practice to consult continually with the direct delegates of the independent, self-managed basic units, then the worker does not need a parliament organized along the lines of the classical party system. Genuine self-management relations assure the permanent and direct participation of associated labor in decision-making at all levels, both in the organs of self-management and in the state organs.

This requires a number of basic changes in the present sociopolitical system. Among other things, these must assure to the Socialist Alliance of the Working People of Yugoslavia and to the Trade Union Federation a more important role in the composition and function of the assemblies. This implies also major reforms in the electoral system. The system of delegations, now implemented only partially, will have to definitely replace the remnants of the system of classical "general representatives."

THE ROLE OF LOCAL COMMUNES, PROVINCES, AND REPUBLICS

The question as to what degree the commune has really become a self-governing community of working people is of critical importance for the proper functioning of the assembly system based on workers' self-management. For the relationships in the commune determine the workers' decisive participation in decision-making, not only in the commune itself but also at higher levels of government.

The commune is the place where the interests of the working people are reflected most directly, both in terms of economics and in regard to the fulfillment of their social, cultural, and other requirements. And precisely because the workers are so directly and tangibly involved, a high degree of self-organization in the commune is necessary so that they can really exercise their right to self-management and proceed on the road toward further democratization of social relations. The commune is the basis for the integration of the workers' self-management system.

Thus the commune should not be considered in isolation, but rather within the context of the entire self-governing structure of Yugoslav society. In fact, self-government in the commune is exercised in the self-managing working organizations and larger integrated units, in the local communities and communities of interest, as well as in the sociopolitical organizations. The commune assembly is the link between and expression of interaction of these mechanisms of self-management.

Sociopolitical relations in the autonomous provinces and republics are articulated in a similar way, and this applies to the federal level as well. It is essential to ensure that associated labor exercises its influence at all these levels.

There is no doubt that the further strengthening and development of the system of self-management is a precondition for the internal political stability and unity of the country. It is also an important factor in her external relations, based on independence and cooperation with all democratic and progressive forces in the world which are ready to cooperate on terms of mutual respect.

Within these broad guidelines, however, the development of the theory and practice of self-management has not followed, and cannot follow, one straight unswerving line. There are subjective and objective limitations; problems, tasks, and priorities keep shifting.

Thus, during the first period, the foremost task was to strengthen the autonomy of the working units (departments) in the enterprises. Today, by contrast, attention is focused on the large, integrated economic enterprises, and national unities.

THE IMPACT OF SELF-MANAGEMENT

The idea of workers' self-management, that is, the participation of workers in the management of economic enterprises and in decision-making on all sociopolitical problems, represents a material force today. With varying strength it is coming to the fore on all continents and in all social systems, within national frameworks and in international relations. It manifests itself not only in ideological and political programs but in constitutions and laws.

It is an idea which is opening up a new historical era. The building of the system of self-management in Yugoslavia is a contribution to this development. Thus it is fraught with international implications, regardless of the fact that, measured against the ultimate goal, only the first few steps have been taken.

4

SELF-MANAGEMENT IN YUGOSLAVIA: SOME IMPENDING PROBLEMS

by Dr. Najdan Pasic
*Dean, Faculty of Political Science, Belgrade University
and Chairman, Serbian Delegation to the Federal Parliament*

THE NEED FOR SELF-MANAGEMENT AND ITS MEANING IN YUGOSLAVIA

The complexity of the systems of production and management characterizing contemporary industrial and "post-industrial" society has intensified a widespread feeling of dissatisfaction and resignation. People resent the absence of any real possibility of participating effectively in decision-making and managing affairs directly affecting their existence as workers and social beings. Hence the numerous attempts and projects, initiated by organized labor (trade unions, workers' parties) and other groups, are engendered more or less spontaneously, to solve this problem or at least to ameliorate the situation. Thus various forms of consultation have been established involving workers and office employees and allowing for their participation, even if restricted, in decision-making through workers' councils, production consultations, committees for "joint consultation," enterprise councils, organs for coordination and consensus, and so on.

There is an understandable tendency to interpret the workers' councils in Yugoslavia simply as one of these attempts to improve and humanize labor relations through the participation of the workers in management. This interpretation fails to take note of the broader historical context for the creation of the workers' councils in Yugoslavia, its far-reaching revolutionary effects and implications for the development and character of the sociopolitical system in its entirety.

The very problems which have emerged and which are due to be settled in the course of this stage of development show that the development of self-management in Yugoslavia, in spite of all avoidable and unavoidable waverings and delays, has been a profoundly revolutionary process which has introduced radical changes into the basic social relations and has exerted great influence upon all institutions and all spheres of social life.

Yugoslav society as a whole has reached an absolutely new and original historical situation. Historical evolution has confirmed that self-management cannot be reduced to the limits of a simple reform in the sphere of "industrial relations," introducing certain corrections and improvements into substantially unchanged wage-labor relations between workers and private capital or the state. Self-management represents the socioeconomic and humanitarian transformation of society. The principal challenge of Yugoslav society at this historical juncture is the final transformation of self-management into a complete system of organization of society as a whole.

SOCIAL OWNERSHIP—THE BUILDING BLOCK

Social ownership of the means of production and of other means for pursuing social activities provides the material basis for the relationships of self-management. Property is managed directly by the workers themselves, organized in enterprises and institutions.

In Yugoslavia, as in other socialist countries, the initial form through which private ownership was abolished was state ownership, effectuated through acts of nationalization and expropriation. State ownership, however, created a new power over, and independent of, associated labor. The tremendous social power invested in the state authority facilitated the consolidation of state/wage-labor relationships, depriving the direct producers of the right or possibility of making direct decisions regarding the management of production and the distribution of the results of this work. This monopoly of state ownership, if imposed and maintained on a lasting basis, becomes the principal source of social contradictions and tendencies leading to the growth of bureaucracy throughout the entire social fabric.

The abolition of all forms of alienated economic and political power over people is the historic and human essence of the socialist transformation of society, but no progress toward socialism is attainable without the transformation of state ownership into direct social ownership, which means the abolition of all monopolistic ownership and of all appropriation of rewards on the basis of ownership.

If one considers self-management in the broader historical sense as a system of relationships in which the social process of emancipation of labor is being implemented, self-management is thus indivisibly associated with the transformation of state ownership into social property. The first step in the development of self-management in Yugoslavia coincided—and not by accident—with the first measures designed to restrict and eventually to eliminate the monopoly of state ownership. The legal basis for the formation of workers' councils was provided by the "Law on the Management of State Economic Enterprises and Higher Forms of

Economic Association by the Workers' Collectives," an act which explicitly limited direct state management of the economy and initiated the institutionalization of self-management.

This consistently pursued course of removing state elements from social ownership was implemented further through the increasingly firm and direct association of the right to utilize social property with the exercise of certain decision-making functions by the working people organized in their self-management bodies. In this manner social ownership was to become the universal material foundation for autonomy in terms of self-management. Inherent in this is the assumption that the working man, laboring in association with his fellowworkers and utilizing the socialized means of production, will enjoy a new social position as, by the very act of taking a job, he acquires all the rights and the responsibilities of a self-manager who manages and disposes of the means with which he works. This new production relationship—the foundation for the entire social organization—has been established and is protected by the constitutional order itself. Behind it stands the organized power of the socialist state.

SELF-MANAGEMENT AND THE MARKET SYSTEM

But the self-managing associations are not and cannot be isolated and self-sufficient entities. They are merely the functionally dependent parts of a broader whole—the entire society. Consequently their actual character and nature are determined by the manner in which they establish connections among themselves and with other parts of the social organism, thereby integrating with the whole of society. If the working organizations are to be truly self-managed, if they are to represent the concrete organizational form through which man can secure the real premises for his freedom so that he can directly and effectively make decisions affecting the conditions under which he works and his material existence, then these organizations must be linked up and integrated into a larger whole—into the overall structure of society. This has to be achieved in a way that does not annul their independence in decision-making on all essential questions concerning the exercise of their basic functions. Obviously, the establishment of links and the integration of self-managing associations cannot be effectuated by their incorporation into the hierarchical system of relationships in a centralized, administrative mechanism, whether statal or semistatal.

"Self-management," says Professor Lefebvre, "must also confront and solve the problems of market organization. It is not for it, either in principle or in practice, to negate the law of values. There is no need to pretend that, in its name, the market, enterprise profitability, the law of values in exchange, can be 'transcended.' Only centralized statism had that exaggerated ambition."[1]

The Yugoslav experience completely confirms this concept. As self-management evolved into an overall system of social organization, it constantly pursued the course of replacing the system of administrative centralization with self-managing organizations operating in the market under suitable forms of commodity-money exchange.

Exchange through the medium of the market, grounded in the law of values, provides an objective criterion for realizing the basic socialist principle of income distribution.

First of all, within a market mechanism, the associated producers (self-management units) are free from the arbitrary exercise of power by "outside" factors which could distort distribution for their own ends.

Second, earning income through market exchange rather than through sheer administrative distribution engenders a considerable impulse to economic development and raises labor productivity which serves the workers' personal and social interests.

Third, operating within a market system renders the self-managed working organizations more independent, and makes them the principal investors in the expansion of productive forces throughout society as a whole. The very fact that each working collective, each self-managed organization within the framework of legally established rights and responsibilities, earns and distributes income independently and makes decisions on personal earnings and on the expansion of production via investments, creates a system of relations in which the self-managing worker is really in a position to manage directly the results of his labor. Thus the key question of freedom and democracy for every society in which private ownership has been abolished, the question of who will acquire the power resulting from the management and disposal of socialized means of production, is solved through the market mechanism in a manner benefiting the associated workers themselves rather than political forces and factors that make decisions in the workers' name.

The concrete historical process of transforming self-management into an overall system of social organization must be based—at least as indicated by the Yugoslav experience—on the independent position of the self-managing working organizations which make free use of certain socialized means of production and freely create and distribute income as independent commodity producers. Such a system will secure (1) the abolition of, or at least, an essential restriction on, the fundamental forms of economic power wielded by the bureaucracy over the working class; and (2) the strengthening of the position of the worker in the sphere of managing social production and distribution, which quantitatively expands and qualitatively alters his opportunities for active participation in political decision-making not only within local frameworks but also on a broader social plane.

FROM INDUSTRIAL TO POLITICAL DEMOCRACY

The new position of associated labor established on self-management was the principal source of the creative energy which brought about far-reaching transformations in the economic structure and the system of political relations. Changes in both spheres were dynamic and radical and thus attest to the revolutionary substance of the new production relationships based on self-management.

The creation of workers' councils and the development of self-management in the sphere of material production initiated a comprehensive process of paring down the role of the state and freed social forces from their subordination to alienated political forces personified in the state.

An important and concrete aspect of this process was the introduction of organs of self-management and social management in the schools, cultural-scientific and health institutions, social insurance services, housing, and, generally, in the entire service sector of the economy, with the exception of the army and the state administration in the narrowest sense of the word.

There are two types of decision-making bodies in the self-managing organizations within the service sectors. One type is elected directly by the persons employed in the given working organization; the other consists partially or wholly of delegates of the citizens concerned, or of the community at large. This setup was designed to ensure that executive government bodies would not interfere in the process of coordination of the interests of people engaged in a certain activity or pursuing an interest of the community at large. Abolition of direct state management of these spheres of service leaves room for voluntary mobilization of social resources and energy and promotes the position of the working people in their capacity as self-managers even outside the sphere of material production. Management of these spheres of the life of society and of social activities is thus placed under democratic control of the citizens, associated in self-management. They set aside part of their income to finance certain social and public services in their own and in the broader public interest.

THE WITHERING AWAY OF THE PARTY APPARATUS

An important aspect of the political system is the institution of direct democratic decision-making and participation in policy-formation through assemblies of voters in parts of the territory of the local communities, assemblies of working people in the enterprises and institutions, assemblies of those who utilize the services of communal and other enterprises, referendums in the working organizations and in the sociopolitical communities, etc.

Another component in the process of developing direct democracy is the commune which is the basic sociopolitical form of territorial integration of self-management and the organ of political power of the working people.

Finally, the replacement of the political-representative system by the system of direct democracy is reflected in changes in the character of the mandate of deputies and councilmen. If the representative bodies are to shed their parliamentary features and acquire the character of working bodies, they must be composed not only of independent political representatives but also of delegates who retain firm links with the self-managing structures. As a rule, these deputies of large working communities remain at their jobs in their working organizations.

All these are elements reflecting essential changes in the nature of the deputy's mandate, designed to ensure that the assemblies have a self-managed, directly democratic and working character rather than being political representative and parliamentary bodies.

This change in the concept of the deputy's mandate goes hand in hand with a change in the character and role of the political organizations, particularly the political parties.

The first indications of this change go back to the early years of development of self-management and the formation of workers' councils in the enterprises. The Communist Party itself soon became aware of the changes this implied. At the Sixth Congress of the Communist Party of Yugoslavia in 1952, only two years after the promulgation of the Law turning state enterprises over to the management of working collectives, decisions were adopted mapping out the transformation of the Party. The Party ceased to be the center and backbone of a system of all-embracing and direct state management; it became an ideological and political force acting as an integral part of the system of self-management and in accordance with democratic principles. Thus the process of transforming the Communist Party into the League of Communists had begun.

In working toward the goal of reintegrating society through self-management, particularly important roles have been assigned to the assembly system. At all levels, from the commune to the federation, the assemblies derive directly from the self-managing social base and remain linked with it in discharging their functions. While they exercise the functions and have the characteristics of supreme organs of political power in a specific territory, they are, at the same time, a form of self-managing organization of labor in the sphere of managing joint social affairs.

Systems founded on capitalist, private-property relationships could provide the basis only for indirect, political representative democracy embodied in representative institutions of the parliamentary type. Under capitalism, the formally free citizen-voter holds a passive position in the process of political decision-making, which corresponds to the subordinate, wage-labor position he occupies in the economic sphere and, in general, to the separation of the public from the private spheres of social life.

Systems based on state-ownership monopoly can give rise only to the type of representative institutions which, irrespective of formal normative measures, are actually under the domination of the state-party executive and its apparatus, in accordance with the dictates of direct state management of the processes of production and distribution.

In contrast to this, the system based on advanced self-managing relationships requires that representative institutions, the organs of state-political decision-making, be constituted in their structure and functions as a direct extension and expansion of the self-managing organization of labor.

THE STRUCTURE AND ROLE OF THE LEGISLATIVE FUNCTION OF GOVERNMENT

The multicameral structure of the assemblies (from the communes to the federation) makes it possible for various spheres of the self-managing organizations to be adequately and equally represented in political decision-making and in the entire work of the assembly. According to the Constitution of 1963 and the pertinent constitutional amendments, the Federal Assembly has five chambers. Three of these represent self-managing organizations in the areas of economy, education and culture, and health and social insurance. The fourth, or sociopolitical chamber, is elected directly by the citizens in the communes, and the fifth, the chamber of nationalities, consists of deputies delegated by the assemblies of the republics and provinces on a basis of equality. The structure of this chamber thus ensures the participation of the republics and provinces, that is, of the various peoples and nationalities of Yugoslavia, on a footing of equality with the other chambers (which represent nonterritorial functional interests and forces) in the policy-making of the Federation.

Problem Areas

The development of society along practically unexplored historical paths has yielded easily discernible positive results in the sense of democratizing social relations and ridding them of statist hindrances and framework. However, while proceeding along this path Yugoslav society has come up very directly, not only in theory but in daily practice as well, against contradictions and problems that differ substantially from those confronting both capitalist society and the system of administrative socialism.

CAPITAL CONCENTRATION:

The first and most crucial problem is how to control the concentration of "social capital," that is, to facilitate its mobility according to laws of the modern market economy while still keeping it under the effective control of the workers themselves. The concentration of capital Yugoslavia has been experiencing lately creates internal contradictions and tensions in the system and has a negative effect on self-management relations even where they have already taken root, as in industrial organizations. This concentration of capital tends to strengthen inordinately the position of the professional political-managerial stratum (in its mediatory and patronizing role) while, on the other hand, it kindles technocratic tendencies within individual enterprises, especially in the big integrated entities; for in such a situation of economic insecurity and dependence upon external factors beyond their control, workers are often willing to give discretion to the professional-technical management or to the stratum which is termed "technostructure" in the contemporary economic and sociological literature.

If self-management is to overcome these bureaucratic-statist and technocratic obstacles and if it is to be able to survive as a social reality instead of being reduced to a normative facade behind which different factual relationships are hidden, it is absolutely necessary that it should develop into a uniform system of global social organization. The problem in fact boils down to the question of how to ensure that the process of capital investments and the distribution of benefits derived from these investments be placed under the direct and real control of the constituents of each working organization. This is the "to be or not to be" question of the self-management system today.

There are several constitutional amendments that address themselves to the solution of this key question. Constitutional Amendment XXI establishes that "socialist self-management relations are founded on the socio-economic position of the working man in social reproduction which guarantees to him the realization of his own material and moral interest while working with the means of reproduction owned by society and making decisions directly and on an equal footing with other workingmen in collective work, about all affairs of social reproduction."

This basic principle is even more directly expressed in Amendment XXII which states that "it is the inalienable right of workers to manage affairs and means of social reproduction on the basis of their work and to decide on the income produced by the basic organization of collective work to which they belong."

Naturally, constitutional amendments are not confined solely to establishing and formulating attitudes. They also determine the methods and instruments for the realization of the principles they proclaim.

The constitution regulates the position and role of the basic working organizations both within the framework of enterprises and within broader organizational entities. It furthermore regulates the total process of social production, trade, and distribution. Finally, it determines the character and content of the so-called "self-management accords."

The Constitution conceives of the basic organization of collective work as the prime cell of the self-management system, the primary form of Marx's "free association of producers." In these organizations the workers exercise directly, without external mediators such as the state or the market, their fundamental self-management right to decide on all questions of their collective work and, on the basis of this work, to distribute the total income which represents the socially (on the market) confirmed result of this work.

This is why the Constitution guarantees that "workers in every part of the work organization (enterprise, institution, etc.) in which the result of their collective work can be confirmed as a value on the market or in a work organization and which can be freely expressed on this basis, have the right to organize such a part as a basic organization of collective work."

Any income resulting from the pooling of work and funds (in the form of interest on credit or in some other form) "is a component part of the income which basic organizations of collective works produce" and this means that the workers decide on the use of this part of the income directly within the framework of self-management.

This guarantees that the workers themselves decide on the question of the concentration and circulation of the means of social reproduction. It also provides a substantial guarantee for the preservation of self-management sovereignty and the equality of workers within the framework of the enterprise and within the broader integrated entities.

Even within the context of the so-called "large systems," no matter how complex, the basic rights of decision-making are assured to every worker, from the bottom up. By securing the appropriation of income on the basis of work done as objectively verified through the market mechanism, the basic organizations of collective work are enabled to withstand bureaucratic subjectivism and arbitrariness. At the present stage of development this is a vital condition for the de-statization of production relations and the affirmation of workers in the role of self-management.

SELF-MANAGEMENT ACCORDS:

It is evident that an economic system consisting of independent molecules of basic organizations connected only through the market could lead to an anarchic market, where great and continuously growing inequality in the material position of basic organizations of collective work and of entire branches and regions would evolve. As a final consequence, this would entail the establishment of group-ownership relations, conducive to a restoration of class struggle with all that this entails.

Hence the great significance of the "self-management accords." These are agreements which organizations and communities conclude between themselves for the independent regulation of a whole range of vital socioeconomic relations. Among other things, they establish the criteria for the internal distribution of income within the basic organizations of collective work, and regulate the mutual relations among these organizations and the various forms of pooling labor and capital. They also regulate the mutual obligations between the workers in the service sector (health service, education, etc.) and the users of these services. Self-management agreements define precisely the obligations of work organizations, in keeping with the principles of reciprocity and solidarity, to help organizations which are experiencing exceptional economic difficulties and to set aside funds for the employment, job retraining, and realization of the rights acquired by the workers, when because of technological and economic reasons, the organization in which they had been working no longer needs their work.

THE ROLE OF THE STATE:

What happens in the event that self-management accords and social agreements are not concluded or honored? In this event it is possible to establish under law the measures which regulate those relations which have not been regulated in a self-management accord or social agreement. It may also be stipulated that a precedent, corresponding social agreement will be applied. Similarly it is possible to limit provisionally under law the use of the part of funds of social reproduction or to establish the obligation to pool these funds for the sake of financing certain absolutely necessary requirements of social reproduction.

Consequently, even under the latest changes which the constitutional amendments contain, the state is not absolutely excluded from the process of expanded reproduction but its role is far more consistently reduced to the securing of general conditions and guarantees for the functioning of the self-management mechanism which is ever more independently and in

increasingly greater spheres regulating basic relations in the process of expanded reproduction and is securing its socialist line and contents.

Under all these measures one has naturally not eliminated or transcended all the basic social contradictions that are inherent to commodity
production and to distribution according to the work invested. Commodity production requires a state even under our new relations.
Whether, due to this and in this setting, bureaucracy and technocracy and
social forces which are their vehicles will be further strengthened, or
whether the forces which are the vehicles of self-management and
democratic relations will be consolidated depends, among other things,
upon the manner in which these contradictions will be solved. Unless we
find a method for creating a self-management basis for this, we shall not
be able to develop the social basis for transcending bureaucracy. . . . The
de-statization of economic relations in the sphere of production and
distribution of values, in the sphere of expanded reproduction—for which
constitutional-legal foundations have been given in Amendments XXI and
XXII—is the point of departure for the full de-statization of socioeconomic life and for the de-bureaucratization of political life.[2]

THE PROCESS OF SELF-MANAGEMENT

The liberation of work is a distant historical prospect in which scien-
tifically perceived possibilities are necessarily intermingled with elements
of social utopianism. Consequently, it is a vision into which are projected
some of the most progressive aspirations of contemporary man, but it is
not the reality of today or tomorrow. However, self-management brings
this vision closer, offering possibilities for a clearer perception of the paths
in this direction and of the obstacles besetting these paths.

Society cannot yet live without political authority, but the development of self-management makes it possible and makes it necessary that
this authority be as directly as possible under the control of collective work
and that it be integrated into the structures and processes of self-
management decision-making from the bottom up. This means, in fact,
the development of a democratic political system which makes possible
the expression and free articulation of various interests based on the
existing differences in society while, at the same time, offering a
mechanism of selection and guidance which secures the advantage and
supremacy of long-term socialist interests. Historical experience shows
that it is possible to develop such a system even in an economically not yet
highly developed country such as Yugoslavia.

NOTES

1.   Henri Lefebvre, "Problems theoriques de l'autogestion," in *Autogestion*, No. 1, Decem-
      ber, 1966.

2.   From Milentije Popovic's speech at the joint session of all Chambers of the Federal
      Assembly held on March 29, 1971, quoted from *The Constitution of the Socialist
      Federalist Republic of Yugoslavia*, 1971, pp. 21-23.

5

SELF-MANAGEMENT: THE EXPERIENCE AND THE RESULTS

By Joze Pacek
Secretary, Slovenian Parliament

IN June 1950 the first law for industrial self-management was adopted in Yugoslavia. Accepted under the banner of "Factories for the Workers," the law ensured the rights of workers in the administration of most industries and business enterprises. By 1956 the self-management system had passed its organizational stage and was firmly established in the economic structure of the country. By May 1971 when the second Congress of Self-Managers was held, self-management had grown to include schools, hospitals, and housing developments. Nearly two-thirds of the total labor force have been, in the past twenty years, elected to different kinds of self-management organs. This indicates that self-management began to serve as a mechanism for worker involvement in industrial management as well as a system of citizen participation and the foundation of the Yugoslav sociopolitical system.

The road to this point of development was not smooth, being marked by a number of wrong turns and littered with obstacles. At the factory level, self-management was confronted with problems of poorly developed democratic attitudes, conservative work habits, insufficient education, and conflicts of interest between skilled and unskilled labor, to mention only a few. On a larger scale the problems of statism, bureaucracy, technocracy, and elitism continually presented themselves. To cope with these obstacles, the self-management system had to be modified and reinforced many times. Even so, many of the problems still exist, although it is unlikely that any young socioeconomic system can expect total or immediate success against such pervasive problems. Nevertheless, those key qualities which seem to be essential for long-term success, those of flexibility and creativity in accommodating to the changing needs and demands of society, have been shown to be present in self-management.

Self-management's strongest criticism, however, did not come from those skeptical of its potential for social change, but rather from those who doubted its workability as a consistent system of production. Because the short-range interest of workers does not take into consideration broad social and technological developments, it was feared that the new system would entail a loss in productivity and an eventual stagnation of the economy.

This fear, it seems, was unfounded. Overall productivity throughout the economy has more than tripled during the twenty years of self-management. Industrial productivity has increased at a rate of 10 percent a year. The standard of living has risen to four times its previous level and helped to decrease the peasant population of Yugoslavia over 20 percent. In fact, Yugoslavia, which has been an underdeveloped country, has succeeded in reducing the economic development gap between itself and the industrialized nations. It must be noted that this development has been done without severely limiting market mechanisms via central planning, for to have done so would have hindered the development of modern enterprises and perhaps lowered overall productivity. It is doubtful whether there could have been such a marked rate of economic development without the simultaneous introduction of modern technology and advanced forms of marketing systems, along with self-management. The claim, however, that self-management would hinder productivity was certainly not borne out. In fact the major difficulties in economic development have arisen in just those periods when self-management was not being implemented fast enough.

The theory that workers are not interested in broad social and technological developments also had to be modified under self-management. The results of a questionnaire filled in by industrial workers in the Republic of Slovenia revealed that workers do not make decisions based on their perceptions of socioeconomic phenomena. In 1965 when an exaggerated inflation had necessitated economic reforms, only 45 percent of the workers who filled in the questionnaire saw the possibility of increased wages through increased production, while the majority favored either a price increase or a reduction in investments. A year later when economic reform was in full swing, 73 percent of the workers favored an increase in production to raise personal income. In 1967 when the effects of the exaggerated inflation had begun to decrease, 71 percent were of the above opinion. The workers in this case were ready to support envisaged social aims where they saw truly documented needs to be at stake. It is not surprising, therefore, that a resolution was adopted at the recent congress of self-managers instituting the obligatory dissemination of information on significant questions concerning the economy of the enterprise and the society at large. It was stressed that this information is necessary to aid the workers in enlightened decision-making and therefore should not be under the exclusive control of the leading personnel of the enterprise.

It should be mentioned here that in spite of self-management there have been strikes in Yugoslavia. Also, in several cases when enterprises were showing a loss, compulsory administrative measures had to be introduced; and there are still some enterprises in which self-management is only an external facade for inner autocratic decision-making by a small group of leading personnel. By understanding the factors that influence socioeconomic development and relations not only in Yugoslavia but in other countries as well, such as structural discordance, nonliquidity, unemployment, uncertainties generated by the market, etc., we can better gauge self-management in these instances of failure. The analyses to date have agreed on one major answer: in each case of failure, the development of self-management was lagging behind, either with respect to the overall economic system or in specific organizational forms. In fact, whenever self-management was not developing into a complete system of social, economic, and political relations, it has had to be helped along by imposed social action. In each case, however, these actions, whether"imposed administrative measure," constitutional changes, or steps taken by trade unions, have been directed toward the further development and growth of self-management. After considering the problems, the recent Congress of Self-Management passed a generally accepted resolution urging that such measures be abolished whenever possible, thus giving rise to a form of self-management in which the workingman will be the real bearer of problem-solving responsibility in production and social relations, and the material basis of self-management will be strengthened.

One of the key reasons for the success of self-management in Yugoslavia has been the willingness to make broad constitutional changes to accommodate self-management's expanding role in the society. This year alone, twenty amendments to the federal constitution of the republics were passed. Although these amendments, generally directed towards giving individual workers greater control over the acquisition and investment of his income, will not be immediately implemented, they do signify a major commitment to the continued expansion of self-management.

One of the most difficult problems that the new amendments have attempted to deal with is the creation of a mechanism through which the individual worker can exercise control over the income he has earned for his past work. Because the society as a whole depends on continual reinvestment of capital derived from profits, private accumulation is not permitted. The worker can, however, determine to some extent where his surplus income will be invested, either in his own enterprise or into profitable outside enterprises. This is not a classical shareholder relationship where profit is a permanent source of acquiring income but rather one in which profit is acquired on the basis of mutual risk and represents the amortization of invested capital.

The same principles apply to foreign capital investments and though such investments remain small, the level of commitment to this new system has been indicated and will encourage future investments.

Self-management in Yugoslavia seems to have established itself as a successful and important socioeconomic system. It has done this by meeting, and successfully adapting itself to many serious challenges; but the real test for self-management, indeed the real test for all existing socioeconomic systems, is yet to come. With the rapid development of technology and industrialization it is now clearly evident that the whole structure of work and its related patterns will soon undergo a dramatic change. The increase in overall standards of living and decline of physical work will bring about an increased emphasis on creative incentives and cultural affirmation in work. It is just this view of future developments that offers the most hope for the long-term success of self-management. Its potential for application on all levels of human activity from production to education to art, and its ability to provide higher rewards than mere economic ones for those it serves will be strong assets in a world of changing needs. The challenge to self-management is to provide for its own evolution and growth.

6

INDUSTRIAL DEMOCRACY AS A COMPONENT IN SOCIAL CHANGE: THE ISRAELI APPROACH AND EXPERIENCE

By Yehuda Yudin

Chairman of Workers' Participation in Management Department
General Federation of Labor in Israel-Histadrut

HISTORICAL BACKGROUND

THE process of social development in Israel laid the foundations for the establishment of an economic democracy. The pioneer generation founders of the new State built a labor economy from a vacuum. There was no nationalization of an economy based and developed on private capital, but rather the creation of a new labor economy founded and managed by workers. In fact, this was the way of the development of a considerable and important part of the national economy of Israel.

The historical conditions of immigration to an underdeveloped country with a hostile political regime in the years preceding the independence of the State turned the creation of an independent economy by poor immigrants into a supreme national need. As a rule, this was also the only way to work, settle down, make a living, and protect the physical welfare of the family and the small community. The feeling of national need was combined with the recognition of the social and socialist uniqueness and destiny.

The Labor Movement had a dual test: the creation of an economy by the inexperienced hands of the workers, absorbed in unfamiliar trades; and the undertaking of independent management, finances, production, marketing, and distribution of income. Simultaneously, each enterprise in this economy was also to constitute a nucleus of a society according to socialist norms and ideological criteria set by the community. In the regulations of the kibbutz, the moshav, cooperative movement and the administrative economy, the uniqueness of each framework left its stamp, but socialist ideals ran through the history of each as a leitmotif.

THE ISRAELI SELF-MANAGED ECONOMY — AN
EXPRESSION OF IDEOLOGICAL BELIEFS
AND ECONOMIC AND SOCIAL NECESSITIES

The creative process of building the independent Labor Economy flowed from the very beginning, long before the establishment of the State of Israel, through various channels. Groups of young pioneers, immigrants and workers strove to express their beliefs and expectations in different ways and shaped the forms and contents of their communal life. All of them were united around one general objective—the creation of a new Jewish workers' society in the ancient homeland—but differed from one another in their views of the shape which the new ideal society should take and in their assessment of the educational and political ways leading to the goal at which they were aiming.

The young working class was united in the fundamental belief that the Labor Movement must assume central responsibility for developing and building up the country and preparing conditions for economic, social, and cultural absorption of the masses of new immigrants (olim) returning to their Homeland. Yet separate groups—whether political parties or youth movements—jealously maintained their own sets of values. Among those who looked at agricultural work on the land as the chief way to normalization of the economic structure of Jewish life and its "productivisation,"the debate stormed between those who believed in the collective (Kibbutz) and those who strove to live in cooperatives of individuals (Moshav Ovdim); between the large "open" Kibbutz and the "organic" intimate "Kvutza."

In the producers' cooperatives in the towns the debate has never ceased as to the optimal dimensions for the growth of the economic units, heated by the constant fear of giving away the sacred principle of not exploiting any hired labor.

The consumer cooperative has discussed whether it should turn toward the entire population or serve only its own closed ring of members.

All these permanent schisms reflected the awareness of the Israeli organized Labor Movement of the direction and weight of Labor Economy in the general development of a workers' society. However, not less complicated have been the problems which besieged the other part of the independent Labor Economy, the so-called administrative sector, which is owned directly by the Histadrut (General Federation of Labor in Israel)[1] and managed by its institutions. This section grew out of the necessity to combine the entire force of will of the whole movement toward some of the major objectives of national and social importance—creation of new branches of the economy almost unknown by the Jewish workers in the countries from which they originated, such as industry, the building trades, aviation, work at sea, etc. To this end Histadrut assembled people and some capital on a voluntary basis and built a technologically advanced economy of a magnitude unknown in the country before. These indispensable and ever growing activities have been nourished by the central theme in the Israeli Labor Movement's ideology—the theory of synthesis between social struggle and socialist construction, which remains to this day the source of its uniqueness.

It is proper at this point to give a brief account of the specific characteristics of each of the main sections of the Labor Economy in Israel.

The Kibbutz

Being the most radical wing in the search of the "new society," the Kibbutz represents a bold adventure into the socialist future of humanity.

The Kibbutz Movement began when groups of young men and women set out to establish collective agricultural settlements in the then most remote and dangerous parts of the country. The first Kibbutz, Degania, was formed in 1911 at the then desolate point where the river Jordan flows out of the Sea of Galilee. But the great push forward, the foundation of the Kibbutzim (plural for Kibbutz), came with the third large wave of immigration after the First World War. Groups of young people, consisting of members of the "Hechalutz" (Pioneer) Movement and other Zionist-Socialist Youth Movements, began to arrive then in relatively large numbers. Their purpose was not just to live in Israel (then Palestine), but to build by direct spiritual and physical self-effort a new society. This Youth, distinguished by its high intellectual and moral level, achieved wonders in establishing a chain of collective settlements all over the country.

The Kibbutzim have played a decisive role in the Jewish self-defense during the most difficult periods. But they have never been just frontier settlements. Bustling with cultural, ideological, and educational activities, they have also developed the most modern agriculture, which ranks with the most advanced in the world in respect to high yields, quality, and variety of produce and efficient methods of operation.

The Kibbutz is a collective where all property and means of production, building, etc., belong to the members as a whole; and the Kibbutz and its institutions are entitled to represent them in all legal, economic, and social dealings with the Government and the business world. Life in Kibbutz is based on the principle of fullest equality in rights and duties, work and consumption.

The distribution of the income of the Kibbutz between investment and consumption—culture, education, food, clothing, private living, apartments, etc.—is fixed by decision of the members Meeting. This same Meeting, which is the highest authority of the Kibbutz, elects all its institutions which administer the widely varied areas of its life and activities.

The children are educated in communal homes in which they live and learn together. Twelve years of schooling as a minimum education are given to all children without exception. The education is based on an original approach linked closely with the general life in Kibbutz and investment in it is one of the relatively largest of all its expenditures. The Kibbutz Movement has raised a cadre of outstanding educationalists and teachers, and the level of education in its settlements is thought to be the highest in Israel, as it is oriented toward teaching moral and social values no less than toward formal studies.

The life of the children in joint educational homes under the guidance of pedagogues helps to shape the personality of the children, but in no way are they cut off from their families. At the end of the day's work in the Kibbutz, children spend many hours in their parent's apartments, and the family in the Kibbutz is marked by its close unity and stability.

Teams of Kibbutz members in the various branches of work are formed in democratic fashion. Those in charge of the branches are usually elected by the General Meeting of the Kibbutz; the Administering Committees for the branches, engaging a large number of people, are elected by them directly.

During recent years, after Kibbutz had remarkable achievements to show in the development and yield of agriculture, they have begun to invest considerably in developing industries. The purposes are to ensure the technological progress of the settlement, to raise the living standards of its members, to supply places of employment which are better suited to the possibilities of the older members, and to open a new expanse for the talents of the younger generation.

The percentage of young Kibbutz members who are sent to the universities for advanced studies is increasing steadily. This trend is also reflected in the constant increase in the standard of living as well as in the requirements of the menage, which is developing its economy and technological level at an increasing tempo.

The apprehensions formerly widespread about the economic viability of the Kibbutz have proved absolutely false. It has been proved that a Collective which constitutes a social and economic unit, although it lacks the incentive of private property and personal profit, nevertheless develops a motivation that leads it to peaks of involvement, concern, devotion, organization, self-discipline, and efficiency of labor.

The Kibbutz Movement formerly played and still continues to play a significant part in the social and communal life of the country. Its influence can be judged by the number of Kibbutz members among Government Ministers, Parliament (Knesset) Members and Histadrut and Labor Party leaders and activists—a number which is far higher than the relative proportion of Kibbutz members in the total population of Israel.

The Kibbutz lives and develops in its own fashion. Concentrating upon 3½ percent of the population of Israel, it withstands stresses that are created from the proximity of an environment with a different point of view and way of life. The Kibbutz finds new members from the outer world. They come from the cities, from youth movements in Israel and from Zionist Socialist pioneer movements in other countries. At the same time there is a falling away of young people (about 15 percent) who are attracted to urban life.

The ideological front on which the Kibbutz stands in defending the foundations of its life is of vital interest to the entire Community. It is generally held in the Labor Movement in Israel that there is a mutual and inseparable bond between the future of the Kibbutz and the future of the Labor Movement as a dominant force in the public life of the country—and hence the future of the Society in Israel.

The Moshav Ovdim

The Moshav Ovdim expresses another approach which developed within the pioneer generation of those who built up Israel. As against the aspiration to establish the unitary cell of a Socialist society that characterizes the Kibbutz, the members of the Moshav aspire to implement the revolution of the return to work on the land by creating a class of Jewish agriculturists standing on their own feet, holding their own farm units in the Cooperative Villages which function without the exploitation of hired labor.

The Moshvei Ovdim, like the Kibbutzim, were established on land which is the property of the nation. The first group of Moshvei Ovdim, during the period which preceded the establishment of the State of Israel, was distinguished by a high level of idealistic settlers who viewed their enterprise as pioneer national service and part of the planned transformation leading to the establishment of a labor society based on cooperative foundations.

Their villages consist of private land units, and parts which are cultivated by the Moshav as a whole. The individual plots are usually tilled by the owners and their families with widespread mutual aid among the settlers. Production is planned in coordination with the central cooperative institutions with the aim of ensuring maximum possibilities of exploiting the land and the equipment, which is in part (chiefly the heavy equipment) the property of the Cooperative. Marketing of the produce is organized and handled by "Tnuva"—a Cooperative Organization for marketing agricultural produce, which is common to all labor settlements—Kibbutzim and Moshavim alike.

The members of the Moshav receive their requirements of seeds, equipment, and other necessities through the Hamashbit Central Supply Organization, which is also common to all sectors of labor agricultural settlements. The cooperative concentration of purchasing and marketing secures numerous economic advantages to the Moshav, contributing to relative ease and rapid progress toward economic self-sufficiency.

The mass immigration to Israel following the War of Independence turned in part to agriculture and led to the establishment of many new Moshvei Ovdim. Most of the new settlers came from the Ghettos of Arabic-speaking countries, and their adaptation to the land and cooperative social foundations of the Moshav is one of the most gripping chapters in the recent history of Israel.

High level cooperation contributes to the durability of the Moshav in all the fluctuations of economic junctures and natural disasters. In order to preserve the cooperative values in the economic and social existence of the Moshav Ovdim, the National Moshvei Ovdim Movement is taking steps to consolidate the internal rules and regulations of these villages. During recent years there has been a tendency to strengthen these internal rules by a State Law, which will legally ensure the duty of preserving within the Moshav those principles which are democratically decided upon by the members as a whole, such as the social character of the settlement, restrictions upon the sale of land, implementation of majority decisions regarding the bases of economic activities, etc. This Draft Law is opposed by a minority of Moshav residents, who aim to strengthen individual rights at the expense of the Cooperative foundation, and it thus reflects the clash between opposing tendencies in the Israeli society.

The Moshav Shitufi

It is possible that the Moshav Shitufi (collective-cooperative village) came into existence in order to demonstrate the freedom of choice and decision enjoyed by the workers in Israel in choosing their forms of life and the great variety of expression which they give to their constant searches for the framework which is best suited to individual preferences.

Twenty-two villages in Israel are established on the combined basis of collective ownership of all means of production (like the Kibbutz) and absolutely individual consumption within the family setting (like the Moshav Ovdim). Plans for investments, organization of work, adoption of resolutions regarding the allocation of resources for development of the menage, and current consumption are all decided in the Moshav Shitufi by the members of the group.

The Moshav Shitufi is also responsible for the services of the entire village, such as education, watchmen, health, etc.

In contrast to the organization of economic activities which fundamentally resembles that of the Kibbutz, the situation differs in respect to consumption, the use made of the member's share of the general income, and the organization of the family as an independent consumer unit.

The portion allocated for consumption passes to the family, and the use made of it is left to its free and exclusive decision. The family conducts its own household and shares its private budget among the various items of expenditure as it sees fit.

Although the experience of the various Moshavim Shitufiyim in Israel prove their capacity for handling their problems, and although they have achieved general approval of their right to go their own way within the independent creativity of Israel workers, their relatively small number evidences their basic deficiency. People tend to make a more decisive decision in selecting their way of life. The person who tends towards the Kibbutz aspires to an atmosphere of mutual responsibility and security, and a maximum equality in all fields of life. On the other hand a person tending towards the exploitation of individual free initiative aspires to test and prove his own capacity and correct judgment precisely in the area of economic activity, and he therefore supports the typical Moshav Ovdim.

It is still too early to draw conclusions regarding the rootedness, stability and "worthwhileness" of the various forms of independent labor settlements in Israel. It may be assumed that no "objective" evaluation of this matter will perhaps ever be achieved. An economic creation whose roots are embedded in a yearning for social renewal will always find new votaries who are prepared to bear the yoke. Powerful ideological maturation is capable, as the Kibbutz experience in particular has proved, of working wonders in the field of economics as well, giving rise to unimagined results. There can be no doubt that the social, ideological and economic creation in all its varieties will maintain itself and renew itself from time to time, serving as a source of inspiration to all the workers of Israel.

The Cooperative Movement

Consumer Cooperation in Israel in the fields of commerce, credit, marketing and supply plays a very important part. Thus there is Hamashbir, a comprehensive supply Organization for agricultural settlement, and Tnuva which markets agricultural produce. Through such bodies cooperation is a natural continuation of the producer cooperation, from which its growth and large-scale dimensions derive.

Recently, following a period of stagnation, consumer cooperation has made considerable advances in the service of the urban population. With the entry of modern commercial methods into Israel, the cooperative network has opened Supermarket types of shops in an increasing number of towns and residential areas. Their purpose, as usual, is to ensure that the Community can obtain high quality produce at a reasonable price, and these are indeed popular among consumers. At the same time it must be pointed out that these shops are primarily intended for the general public. They belong to the economic system, the Histadrut, but depend on only a relatively small number of members of the Cooperative Consumer Societies.

There was a time when producer cooperation progressed very well and successfully in Israel. Producer cooperatives were established and flourished in branches like textiles, printing, glass-making and building. They combined joint ownership of the means of production and property with absolute joint responsibility in execution and independent private lives on the part of the members.

This kind of cooperation developed in motor transport in particular. Cooperatives for transport by lorry are among the important factors in this branch, but the greatest success of cooperation has been achieved in the organizing of passenger transport. From modest beginnings about fifty years ago, this has reached the point where all urban and inter-urban transport by motor busses is handled by two Cooperatives, Egged and Dan, which have about 8,000 members together. In spite of the economic difficulties, deriving largely from their rapid rate of development on account of the population increase, these two Cooperatives provide regular transport responsibly organized and (relative to many other countries) cheap, to the inhabitants of the country. It is doubtful whether any private or state organization could have achieved the efficiency and economy which characterizes this cooperative sector.

The rapid development, particularly after the establishment of the State and the commencement of mass immigration, has placed before the cooperatives expansion pressures which were accompanied with no few social problems. In the Kibbutz the joining of new members is not conditioned by the introduction of any money whatsoever as a condition for admission to all rights. In the admission of new members to producer cooperatives in urban districts, however, the acquisition of a "share" is a necessary prerequisite. The amount of the "share" is fixed by an assessment of the cost of property, and requires the approval of the Histadrut Institutions, in order to check any manifestation of speculative exploitation of various situations. Although the approval of candidates for membership in producer cooperatives depends on a Members' Meeting, it is clear that the need for acquiring a share leads to selection on the basis of financial capacity as well. In this branch of cooperation this defect is possibly unavoidable, but it does not facilitate the solution of social problems, particularly when discussing the admission of the hired workers into full membership in the cooperatives, which is the constant demand of the Histadrut.

Cooperation in the Arab Villages

This survey of cooperation in Israel cannot be concluded without referring to the beginnings of the Cooperative Movement in Arab villages. Since the establishment of the State of Israel, 159 Arab Cooperatives have been established, chiefly in the fields of water supply, tilling the soil, purchasing and maintaining mechanical equipment, etc. No small part of the Arab producers in agriculture is associated with the Histadrut Cooperative supply and marketing system.

The penetration of the cooperative idea into Arab villages reflects the deep changes in forms of life and work which used to be traditional in this Community. This transformation has not come about by itself; it has been accompanied by conflict between the traditional viewpoint and the needs of progress deriving from the growing influence of the mutual relations between the Jews and Arabs in Israel. Cooperative development undoubtedly plays a considerable part in raising the living standards of the Arab village and encouraging its social progress. It is through this channel that the idea of workers' self-managed economy takes its first shape in the Arab environment.

Problems and Concerns in the Cooperative, Community System

In confrontation between the principles and realities, the idea of work without exploitation of others, i.e., the prohibition of the employment of hired labor within the Kibbutz and Cooperative Labor Economy, runs like a scarlet thread through the ideological approach and appears in the written Constitution of both Kibbutz and Moshav. However, the great economic success of the independent economy places before it the lure of employing hired workers from outside, in order to satisfy the needs of the expanding and flourishing enterprise.

The problem is acute in the Moshav Ovdim even more than in the Kibbutz on account of its structure. The individual economic unit, even though it is combined in a cooperative structure and in time of distress enjoys the aid of the whole Moshav, is sometimes greatly influenced by economic pressures. Such a unit is often less subject to social and ideological influences of its movement than the Kibbutz Collective. Problems of hired labor, organized cooperative marketing, acquisition of supplies through the joint organized channels, the use of land in accordance with the declared objectives of the Cooperative village while safeguarding the principles binding on those who lease the land from the nation—all these problems have been accompanying labor settlements for years, and serve as a focus for struggle in which interests clash with ideology. It was impossible to prevent deviations in the course of this tempestuous and rapid development. Whenever any section of the labor economy was under pressure from economic processes such as the inability of the cooperative framework or the settlement movement to supply the market's requirements with the necessary manpower, or by the lure of the unorganized marketing with its greater possibilities of profit, etc., the boundaries were sometimes crossed. But in the last resort and along the whole line, faithfulness to the ideological principles has been preserved not only in the Kibbutz but in the Moshav as well. Nor is it surprising. The combination of guiding principles and practical implementation has justified itself as the only line that is capable of ensuring the continued existence and development of collective and cooperative villages both socially and economically.

Economic developments have tested the nexus between the workers economy and their principles, a process which has not been without social shocks. In part these were the result of difficulties in individual adaptation to new occupations, particularly physical work. The overwhelming majority of new immigrants to Israel found that the transition to the new life involved abandoning old habits and occupations and was not at all easy. What is even more difficult, even when it is based on free personal decision, is the need to adapt oneself to a new social life with its internal qualities, organization, and rhythms.

In the course of time there emerged a problem of the new generations born in the Kibbutz and the Moshav who, upon maturity, sought for ways of expressing themselves within the form of life established by the preceding generation of idealistic founders in accordance with its beliefs. For the most part, this new generation remains faithful to its home and its movement. Many of the labor settlements are already being managed by the children and even the grandchildren of the founders. The younger generation sets its stamp on education, culture, and ideology, but this process is not without suffering, hardship, and even departures and withdrawal. Between 15 percent and 20 percent of the younger generation leave the Kibbutzim. Considering the differences between the individualistic city and the collective village which certainly involves qualitative dimensions, this proportion cannot be regarded as unreasonable. In any case, it is interesting to remark that it is lower than the percentage of those educated outside the Kibbutz who join it and leave later.

The labor economy constitutes at present, even when some of the factors responsible for its creation over fifty years ago have altered radically, over 20 percent of the national economy. Its principles did not prevent it from developing a vast and variegated financial ability, and in fact, have facilitated the amassment required for achieving modern technology. Within this economy the workers gained the experience of self-management and professional ability that they can be proud of. By over-coming—not always easily—confrontations with various pressures at each crossroad, it proved the superiority of and the preference for the social ideal and principle as a guarantee of a thriving and healthy economy, thus constituting an example of voluntary economic democracy which is still unique in the world.

DIRECT HISTADRUT OWNERSHIP: DILEMMA AND SOLUTION

In addition to Kibbutzim and Moshavim, we have in Israel en-terprises owned and managed by the Trade Union, Histadrut. It is distinguished in a number of aspects. Like every other section—kibbutz, moshav, and cooperative—this one was also created by workers through their own responsibility and management. Yet in this section the economy belongs actually and legally to the Histadrut and not to to the persons working within it. It is therefore managed according to the resolution passed in the institutions, or by the persons whom the Histadrut has delegated for the purpose. The actual management is in the hands of managers and managements appointed by the Histadrut, and they are responsible to it. In Histadrut companies such as "Koor," the industrial concern, "Solel Boneh," the construction company, Bank Hapoalim, the workers' bank, Yachin Chakal, a company for the execution of work in agriculture, and in other companies in the various branches of the economy, there are tens of thousands of workers, employees, engineers, and technicians who are hired workers in the enterprises. Admittedly, there is an important essential difference emanating from the status of these people as workers of the Histadrut economy. They do not depend on a wage scale fixed by the traditional complexity of negotiations and collec-tive bargaining between their trade union and their employers. In this im-portant aspect the Histadrut's decision suffices, and it automatically binds all the managements. Yet even this important aspect cannot alter the basic fact that the workers are hired workers, and their rights—numerous though they may be—do not exceed the status granted to hired workers.

Histadrut has come to face this problem not by accident. The creation of the "administrative" economy among the other sectors of the workers' economy resulted from historical circumstances. There was work that could only be carried out, in the volume and momentum required, by means of the collective initiative of all the workers. This could be realized only when based on the responsibility of the Histadrut and its institutions. There were organizational, financial, and practical problems which a limited and relatively small body could not undertake. It was essential to find an outlet for the creative ability and the hunger for employment of the workers, who for various reasons could not organize or get used to the framework of the kibbutz, moshav, or cooperative life.

The executive organizations and the economic industry of the Histadrut came to fulfill these needs and solve the problems which required special organizational tools. Once the labor economy which had been created by the Histadrut reached maturity, once it expanded and branched into numerous spheres, the differentiation started between the persons responsible for management on behalf of the Histadrut and the persons executing their orders within the actual framework of the work. At first this differentiation did not constitute a serious social problem. In a relatively small group of workers, the differences of rank and grading did not result in the creation of separate social frameworks. The problem became a nuisance only when the expansion brought hundreds and thousands of new workers who found established patterns, who came as hired workers and remained in this status even when they advanced professionally and functionally.

This reality of the formation of two levels—the managers and the hired workers—placed the Histadrut under a dual pressure: certain tensions within the labor relations system in its own economy became a constant companion with crises reaching peaks, but without removal of the barriers even in periods of relative calm. What was far more serious was the crisis within the Histadrut with the appearance of the conflict between "the capital" and labor from within, a conflict which undermines the moral and ideological basis of the labor movement. An answer had to be found to this state of affairs, and indeed many attempts had been made to alleviate this social and ideological problem. Various suggestions have been made over the years, some of them with the aim of smoothing over the conflict, and others with the intention of totally obliterating the causes.

To the first group one can attribute the wage policy in the workers' economy, and the method of handling work disputes within. Despite the fact that there are uniform wage scales, the wages and the fringe benefits in Histadrut enterprises are, in fact, higher than in any other part of the economy. There is, as well, a policy which is more liberal in the handling of grading, skill level, permanence in work, etc.

This has been the direct result of the interest of the management and the trade unions in activating their direct influence on the workers' economy, in order to promote better relations and to achieve the advantage of public prestige by granting better conditions than those prevailing in the private market.

The method of handling workers' problems and labor disputes by requiring managers' and workers' committees to appeal to the Histadrut's institutions in all instances was also integrated.

There is no doubt that these means contributed considerably, both to the formation of the standard of living in Histadrut enterprises as well as to the stabilization of relations. But this did not solve the entire problem, and tension was clearly felt during periods of economic slump, when the managements faced crucial decisions which met with the opposition of the workers, as well as in times of inflation and wage rise. Radical and better solutions had to be found—solutions that could alleviate the daily tensions at the same time releasing the Histadrut from the "dual" status in which it found itself, simultaneously an employer and trade union.

One solution was rejected by the majority of the Histadrut members in all the democratic confrontations to date. This was the suggestion to alienate the labor economy from the Histadrut, to release it from the

Histadrut's authority, leaving the Histadrut as a trade union only. This proposal was backed in the twenties only by the extreme left. In recent years it has been backed only by the extreme right, which opposes the class characteristics of the Histadrut. The majority are still of the opinion that the Histadrut has not yet ended its unique role in the development of Israel. In the long run, the existence of the labor economy only strengthens the trade unions, occasionally granting economic basis and supplying it with greater maneuverability for its struggles. The majority believe that the Histadrut cannot begin to dismantle its own economy without damaging the foundation of the Labor society in Israel.

It is therefore obvious that the search for a solution to the problems which weigh upon the Histadrut in relation to this part of the labor economy had to be directed toward extension of industrial democracy and introduction of workers' participation. If this challenge is to be met, then the first task of the Histadrut is to push forward at home.

At the 8th Congress of the Histadrut in 1958, the decision was taken on the participation of workers in the management of Histadrut projects. At the meeting of Histadrut industrial workers which took place at Raanana in 1957, the practical ways for implementing workers' participation in management were outlined.

A resolution was passed on the creation of joint councils in factories as a step toward greater participation and a variety of subjects were to be brought up. In 1964 the Histadrut Council decided on the participation of workers in the management of Histadrut factories, and in 1966 the resolution was passed regarding participation of workers both in management and in profits.

Unfortunately, however, despite the fact that the official resolutions of the Histadrut and its councils and committees indicated growing adherence to the idea of participation, they did not indicate any actual advances in this direction. On the contrary, not only did the Histadrut reach its 10th Congress without any real achievements in this field, but it had to face the first test of disappointments.

The resolutions regarding participation were not executed and the more pressing and demanding they were in style and content, the less effective became their implementation. It was evident that the Histadrut institutions which still retained the economic control over the enterprises were, in fact, losing ideological influence over their managerial staff. The Executive was unable to make the managers realize true cooperation in carrying out the reform they did not agree with and to which they objected. The Histadrut institutions also had doubts about pressing for the implementation of participation by means of enforcing their authority, for fear of a split between themselves and the persons heading the economy, as well as increasing antagonisms within the enterprise. The leadership of the Histadrut recoiled from an attempt to activate thé workers themselves in this dispute beyond a certain limit. Thus, the initiative for participation remained without any active and loyal backers.

Furthermore, the entire attitude toward this issue has been affected, especially after the establishment of the independent State of Israel, by differences of opinion within the Workers' Movement regarding the future of the labor economy. The influence of free "liberal" economy, as found in democratic society in the West, weakened the affinity of fairly large circles to the traditional ideology of the labor movement aimed at independent Labor Economy. Economic problems weighed and pressed heavily and the future of the country began to seem to some, dependent on capital and the managerial team rather than on initiatives of pioneering activities and the attitudes of the workers. Some of the responsibility for the gap between the resolutions regarding workers' participation and its implementation should be attributed to the doubts regarding the old preference of ideology as the driving force in economic development.

However, despite all this, foregoing the way of the Histadrut did not seem possible. In a country where the workers' economy had been created for ideological reasons, and the status of the workers' movement leaned so heavily on the very fact that it was an encompassing framework both to the trade union as well as to the economic and social plan, it was impossible to back out.

Had the Histadrut foregone social reform within its economy, it would have meant that it must forego labor economy as such in the future and its role as one of the main pillars of the labor movement in the country. These were the considerations which brought about the most decisive resolution regarding participation in the 10th Congress of the Histadrut in 1966.

The text of the resolution proposed the creation of joint managements in the enterprises instead of only advisory councils. The workers were to participate not only in management but also in profits, as an expression of their actual involvement in "management and responsibility." To guarantee the execution of the resolution, it was agreed that its implementation would be borne by a special department, directly under the Central Executive, instead of the former organizational arrangements which were found to be unsatisfactory.

We can sum up the assumptions on which Histadrut's resolutions were based when it came to undertake the realization of workers' participation in management as follows:

1) The objective necessity for the existence of a Labor economy aimed at social and economic goals, connected with and interwoven in the Histadrut and sustained by resolution of the Labor Movement. The realization that the workers' economy vitally required the identification of the workers with its aims, as well as their participation in the solution of its problems.

2) The certainty that the very same talent for building and directing an economy, discovered plentifully and convincingly in the Kibbutz and Moshav movements and in cooperatives, may also be found among the workers in the "administrative" economy. The realization that the accumulated experience of self-managed economy will serve the workers when they shoulder an active and actual part in the burden for the existence of the enterprises in the Histadrut concerns, such as "Koor," "Solel Boneh," "Teus," etc. The workers' participation in the administrative economy will serve as a bridge between the patterns of the two parts of Labor economy and bring them closer to each other.

3) Society and the economy must find the way to prevent the alienation between them and the people, as it is impossible to establish a just and better society if man does not feel himself in its center, involved in its complexities, actively influencing its formation. The workers of Israel objectively are ready to assume active attitudes regarding the greater and the immediate circles of the environment—society, the movement, and their places of employment. There is a basis for understanding that participation will enable them to give fuller expression to their personalities as well as to their sense of public responsibility.

4) There is a search in the world for newer methods of economic management, and especially industrial management, based on the involvement of the workers and aimed at closing the gap between political democracy in society and an authoritarian administration in the enterprise. These to a great extent are congruent with the aims of the Histadrut and the labor economy.

5) The development of managerial methods based on the involvement of, and consultation with the workers offers a chance for a sound economy. The follow-up of various attempts in the world (including Israel) to achieve workers' participation in management, by means of establishing joint institutions and the fostering of workers' involvement in the solution of the problems of the economy, indicates grounds for optimism. The fact that some, at least, of the attempts have shown favorable results upholds the view that it is possible to proceed along the route of industrial democracy without endangering the professional and efficient management of the enterprise.

6) The need for combining workers' participation in management with workers' sharing in the profits of the enterprise in order to achieve joint responsibility, judging progress according to clearly defined criteria.

7) The improvement of labor relations will not be obtained by the fostering of "human relations" from above. A part of the just solution to the social and economic requirements of the workers depends on the creation of an atmosphere of mutual trust and responsibility toward joint challenges.

8) The aim of an industrial democracy is to create conditions for actual participation in management. It strives to achieve genuine participation in the process of decision-making, but not merely by representation on Boards. The workers' participation in management will never be effective unless it is based on joint institutions with decision-making ability and managerial authority, namely, joint management. The process of workers' participation in joint management begins with the workers' free consent to participation. Participation in the management of a plant should go "downwards" and encompass all the departments, consultation with the workers, expanding the lines of communication verbally and in writing, encouraging workers' proposals for economy and efficiency.

Above all it is clear that worker participation and industrial democracy are not a defined set of rules to be learned by heart and carried out according to set formulas. It is an experiment born out of social need, which must be put to the test at all levels. The immediate task is to translate the ideological assumptions into reality. We can no longer be satisfied by explaining the need for participation, but must lay theoretical and practical foundations for the creation of joint managements, their regularization, and the solution of problems which such activities must raise.

In Israel, when using the definition of "Industrial Democracy" (or the more general term "Economic Democracy"), we distinctly refer to the participation of workers in the management, that is, in the process of making economic, administrative, financial, organizational, and technical decisions.

Contrary to many other countries, we cannot limit workers' participation solely to such important matters as dismissal of workers, industrial safety, vocational training, fringe benefits, etc., for the simple reason that we assume that the scope of Industrial Democracy is much wider. The trade unions in Israel have a long-established practice of covering all these vital issues by nationwide collective agreements. This is one of the numerous ways in which Histadrut, organizing some 90 percent of Israeli workers in its unions, manifests its strength. Labor relations have naturally been strongly influenced by the fact that the workers in this country are a superbly organized and self-conscious sector of the society, maintaining a wide network of institutions for the provision of social services such as the workers' sick fund, social security funds, mutual aid organization, etc.; by the existence of Labor Economy in towns and villages which combine strength with social, moral, and ideological aspirations; and by the fact that the labor parties have been the backbone and source of strength of all our governments since Israel gained independence.

All these factors have left their strong imprint on the development of the political and social democracy in the country. Both directly and indirectly, they influenced its "industrial climate" providing Labor with a bargaining power, but at the same time charging it with more than its fair share of economic and political responsibility.

All these achievements are the fruits of a long and painful process. The early struggles for organized labor, and for recognition of Histadrut at the plant level were more often than not sharp and difficult (particularly in the private sector of the economy), but for some years now the range of topics covered by collective agreements has been greatly extended in all sectors of the Israeli economy. Labor legislation in the post-independent period has given official, if somewhat belated, recognition to many of the workers' gains.

Furthermore, since 1949, upon Histadrut's initiative, joint productivity and advisory councils were set up by special agreement, in industrial enterprises employing over fifty workers. These councils were authorized to advise on matters of productivity and to determine premiums for production in excess of established norms.

In the face of such a broad scope of workers' rights, workers' participation in Israel has to be directed to the core of the matter—the right to share in the responsibility of decision-making in matters affecting the management and the very existence of the enterprise. When it resolved upon the introduction of workers' participation in management, the 10th

Convention of the Histadrut explicitly stated that it referred to "workers' participation in management, responsibility and profits." A special Department for Participation was set up with the purpose of implementing this resolution, and it is to this end that its efforts have been directed.

The above comments are of special significance when trying to describe the difficulties we encountered in implementing the Histadrut's policy of participation in management. In this connection we should now take a look at the two partners whose attitude is an all-decisive one as concerns the future of participation—the managers on the one hand and the workers themselves on the other.

The Struggle for Implementation— The Attitudes of Management

There is no lack of responsible and capable men within the managerial cadre of the Labor Economy. Many of them are loyal members of the Histadrut and the labor movement. The older members can still recall the early days of the movement and themselves as laborers and pioneers who regarded the creation of the economy as the great national and socialist challenge. These men, as well as the younger generation who followed in their footsteps, tasted the full flavor of the unending and occasionally thankless effort of building an economy and putting in operation plants that were sometimes created for political reasons in disregard of the Colonial Governments, for such things as security needs, for immigration requirements, for shortcomings due to economic crises which shocked the very foundations of the Jewish National Home, but least of all for simple and accepted economic considerations. Their position was not made any easier by the mass immigration to the country after the Independence brought to the factories masses of workers who lacked previous training and work habits in modern industrial plants.

The decision to execute the policy of the Histadrut regarding participation placed before them a difficult test. They had learned to respect the might and rights of the trade unions, even when they did not fully agree with them. It is doubtful whether any one of them would have dreamed of attempting to solve issues of work agreements and customs without joint handling and negotiations with the workers' committees. But parallel to this accepted practice, the process of differentiative functioning went further within the Histadrut economy. The managers concentrated on management while the workers were cut off from the economic responsibility and thus regarded looking after their conditions at work as their sole duty. Theoretically the resolution to obtain the workers' participation in management seemed to turn the wheel back to the early days of the labor economy. In fact a gap had opened between the two periods not merely in the difference of times, but in regard to the vast changes in the objective conditions of the society and the economy and the status and mentality of the people.

A considerable effort is required by the managers to overcome the psychological blocks which prevent them from accepting in good faith the decision regarding the participation of workers. But the Histadrut did not ask the managers to cooperate in the execution of the participation for ideological reasons alone, even though these have been the chief reasons in pushing it. Those managers who were wise enough to look beyond the horizon understood that there are also additional factors for examining the management methods. Simultaneously with the realization of the need for turning the labor economy into more advanced lines of production and technology, considerations had slowly seeped in regarding the administrative methods. It was no secret to them that in Israel and all over the world there is constant criticism of authoritarian regimes in management, and indications appear of switching over to methods based on democratization of the economy and the increasing involvement of the workers. For some of the managers it was as though they had toured the entire world only to discover a treasure under their own doorstep—in that tradition of labor self-managed economy, in the kibbutz, the cooperative movement.

During these years there were countless inquiries into the reservations about participation held by many managers. A serious and prolonged effort was made to prove to skeptics that there is no future to some of the old and tried beliefs. It is no longer obvious that workers "understand nothing about management"; that they have "nothing to contribute to management"; that their participation in management would "create a state of anarchy and destroy discipline." It is not as though these apprehensions are always totally groundless, but the lack of workers' participation and their estrangement from the economy could cause for greater complications. It was a difficult task to win over some of the directors to ideas about participating, despite the fact that time and again it was explained that this change was not aimed against the status or authority of the manager, but rather aimed to define his role as the head and leader, acting with leadership and rallying the collective around himself. It is noteworthy that in a few instances the person responsible for the management of the economy showed greater readiness for the participation of the workers in profits than in actual management. Proposals were also made regarding participation in managerial councils instead of participation in active management.

It is difficult to guess how much more time would have been taken up by this controversy had a clear directive not been finally issued by the Histadrut, in its role as the authority responsible for the labor economy. The conclusions published at the end of the controversy by the General Secretary of the Histadrut in May 1970 established that it is necessary to put up effective joint managements with executive authority in Histadrut industries, in accordance with Histadrut policy which had been defined in the past. This, together with the growing realization that from all possible angles a point of no return has been reached will, it is hoped, pave the way for fruitful collaboration with the management in the future. If this is the case, it would have far-reaching effects beyond the labor economy. The changes will follow in the national-public economy as well as in private industry.

The Workers: Conflict Between Faith and Apprehensions

There is no lack of conflicting feelings among the workers. There are old-timers who still feel an ideological and emotional link to the sources of the self creative economy of "Hevrat Ovdim," who still remember the atmosphere of class and income equality, and above all the genuine identification with the pioneer aims of the task. Similar ideas and feelings are shared by those workers who came with the later waves of immigration and who had gradually integrated into the circle of the labor movement, absorbed its atmosphere and reached a degree of active and essential participation within it.

Even within this group it is possible to encounter a great deal of skepticism toward participation in view of the failures in the period of "advisory councils" and attitudes of the management in the past. Their query is whether the intention now is to have "real participation," and they carefully review the proposed constitution and check every iota.

However, the workers community is not uniform. It contains a wide stratum of people who have found themselves in the labor economy without any previous distinct intention to be there. They are relatively new in the country, and have, in most cases, already undergone a great upheaval that has brought them into work in new occupations and environments. For them, the process of integration was a series of efforts to become accustomed to work, to get decent wages, and to become rooted in the language, culture, and habits of their new-old homeland. Their social integration had often lagged behind the improvement of their standard of living. Despite the fact that they were greatly assisted by the Histadrut, their links and emotional identification with its complicated ideology and unique structure are often still wanting. For many of them the enterprise is merely a place of employment, and the talk about the tasks of Labor Economy are met here and there with a great deal of suspicion. Their horizons do not stretch beyond the immediate tasks of the workers' committee and their union.

The difference in status between managers and workers seems so natural to them that they can still regard participation as some sort of a trap. As strange as it may seem, some of the managers' arguments find a sympathetic ear among them. Why indeed should the workers interfere in managerial issues? Why are they being "pressured" to become involved in matters which do not concern them? The argument that the workers should not exceed the boundaries of immediate struggle for wages and work conditions is closest to their hearts and directs them. It should also be recalled that with regard to participation, the influences of the environment hostile to the labor movement as a whole and its undertakings with socialist values in particular are also reflected. Furthermore, among the "rank and file" workers lurks the suspicion that there is a possibility of career-making at their expense. The joining up of their own representatives with the management seems to many as an opportunity employed specifically with that end in mind. To this one should add also the suspicions of several workers' committees that the representation of workers in management might turn into competitive focus against them in the plant, and not necessarily one that expands and enhances the constructive influence of the trade union.

It is impossible to overcome these reservations by ignoring them. They should be dealt with and met both by information as well as proposals. Not in vain have the activities of the Department of Participation turned to a long-term policy of information and education. The problems of the economy and the trade union, the social aims of the labor economy and the role of the Histadrut, the methods of management combining participation, the ways of increasing satisfaction from work—these together with training for fulfilling the role as representatives of the workers in management filled up the work timetable of the department.

Yet information alone does not solve problems. To eradicate the imaginary or real fears, to increase the workers' self-confidence and prompt them to carry the burden of new responsibility, it was also necessary to mold the framework of participation. A constitution which determined the structure of joint management and the boundaries of its authority set clear and obligatory definitions in order to eliminate any suspicion that "real participation" was again not intended. It was decided that there should be joint managements determining all the affairs of the enterprise starting with basic matters such as the long-range policies, and immediate ones such as actual management and current production.

The resolution that workers' representatives should not "pass the fence" and act as actual full-time managers was essential in reducing fears of career-making. They would continue as workers and employees, laborers and technicians throughout their term in management, and take part in its activities and duties without being cut off from their fellow workers. But throughout there is the guiding intention to turn participation into a functional system engaged in determining the economic issues and in decision-making. The participation is presented as a challenge which requires effort and responsibility, and which at the same time bears the prospect of raising the status of the workers in the undertaking, the level of satisfaction with work, and material share in any economic success. The participation is planned as a powerful lever which should bring about economic and social change in the labor economy. It is based on ideological and theoretical foundations of the labor movement, simultaneously with concepts of advanced management. We have written at length about the negative attitudes of the workers, but that is not the whole story. Genuine democratic discussion bears fruit and brings the people back to the original beliefs of the movement. The workers' organization in the Histadrut economy backed the idea of participation. In twenty-five Histadrut enterprises the workers voted for the establishment of joint managements and for accepting, of their free will, their part in the responsibility for giving the Labor "administrative" economy a new image.

THE FIRST EXPERIENCES WITH PARTICIPATIVE SYSTEMS

The five years which have elapsed since the Histadrut passed the resolutions of renewed experiments in carrying out workers' participation de facto, were complex years from all aspects. The ink on the resolutions had hardly dried when the entire economy in 1966 sank into recession, with part-time work and even total unemployment. At the end of the recession period a chain of reorganization began in Histadrut companies, and it has not yet stopped. Complete frameworks of the economy were remolded, and many company directors were replaced, as well as many factory managers. Throughout this period, discussions about participation and methods for its implementation went on and it was only in the middle of 1971 that they came to an end. Finally the issues were resolved upon the basis of the resolutions of the Histadrut. According to these, joint managements should consist normally of seven—the manager, three members appointed by the company (at least one of them from the local higher managerial staff), and three members elected by the workers, two manual workers and a third from the "white collar" employees. This management is the only decision-making body at the undertaking.

Throughout the controversy the work did not stop in the hope of better days to come, and activities went on continuously on the realization that the only real test of participation, as a component in social outlook and as organizational method in the economy, would come with its practical implementation.

In recent years, Workers' Participation in Management has begun to take shape, to gain experience, to take the first cautious steps toward becoming a reality—not yet on the scale and quality we would desire, but already a tangible beginning. Participation by thirty managements of industrial plans and concerns of "Koor" and "Teuss" and local branches of "Solel Boneh," the largest building society in Israel, and in ten central and divisional managements of the Histadrut companies adds up to a serious attempt to face, in terms of daily life, the problems which have been of much concern to the Histadrut for many years.

We refer to the plants where the workers decided in free ballot to commence participation and to establish Joint Managements. The resultant chain reaction is naturally spreading in ever-widening circles. There is informational, educational, and cultural activity during one-day or more extensive seminars and at meetings; there is a periodical and other publications. This time a vey thorough attempt is being made to transform the theory of participation into practice.

We are aware that the Joint Managements will be constantly scrutinized and the decisive judgment will be given by the results of their actual managerial, economic, and social performance. Among thirty managements with workers' representatives on them at individual undertakings and ten more joint Central Boards of Companies, there are several success stories, and a number of failures (at least temporarily) as well. There are those few who stall purposely and postpone issues from one meeting to the next, like a ship without a helm. Each case has its history, concrete characteristics which provide the key for the explanation of this or that development, but generally speaking, the success or failure depends on the ability of the joint managements to pass four tests:

1) Regular and normal functioning of the management; regular

meetings with well prepared agenda; full and detailed information and accurate reports on execution of former decisions; relevant topics for discussions and decisions; clear summing up of debates and formulation of decisions.

2) Formulation of definite objectives for the plant and individual departments in the frame of the general production program and annual budget. Clarification of technological, economic, and organizational resources to be employed in order to reach the fixed objectives.

3) Regular transfer of information regarding Management's plans and decisions to the employees and workers, and discussion of relevant issues at all levels within the plant, General Meetings, Department gatherings, consultation with foremen and groups of workers involved, joint consideration with Workers' Committees.

4) Introduction of profit-sharing not as a benefit granted "from above" but as an integral part of workers' participation in management, linked to the actual economic performance of the undertaking and not to wages fixed by Trade Union agreements.

In every single one of the Joint Managements these criteria have been applied at least in part. Very few have succeeded in applying them fully. This divergence proves how difficult it is to bring all the factors of the system into full harmony.

The Responsibility of the Managers

It should be clear that the central figure in participation is the plant manager. A manager who supports joint management, or at least "accepts the inevitable," will already know that his earlier apprehensions have been unjustified. The workers have not sent to the joint managements financial geniuses or administrative stars (although it is almost certain that, under appropriate conditions, such are also to be found among them); however, their representatives are anything but ignoramuses in all that affects production in the plant.

Workers' participation is not a disturbing factor in management's deliberations, but an added new dimension in them. Even in cases where the workers concentrate on learning the problems during their first years and contribute little else directly, the plant is gaining because of a new understanding which is developing toward problems and difficulties of the undertaking.

The assessment in almost all of the plants (even of some skeptical managers) is that when the elected representatives of workers join the managements, they show their respect for the topics under discussion and their readiness to study the methods of dealing with them. We have not heard a single complaint of a frivolous or superficial approach, and there have not been any attempts to hide behind the mask of ignorance or use it as a cover for unrealistic suggestions. In some cases the managers complain that the workers' representatives confuse the issues and ask the managements to deal with problems which are the responsibility of the Unions and workers' committees. In these cases the difficulty of preserving the demarcation lines between the responsibilities of the two instruments of workers' representatives—the Workers' Committee or Council and the workers in the Joint Management—was demonstrated. There is no need and no justification for a hermetic separation between them. The problems and their consequences are, more often than not, overlapping; the people who deal with them are members and representatives of the same workers' local community, and in any case, close contacts and joint deliberations must be maintained. Nevertheless, there is a clear distinction between the workers' obligation and task on the joint management and their role in ordinary negotiations with the management on wages, etc. Slowly new, somewhat more complicated but also more fruitful, relationships are taking shape. In general it might be said that participation has contributed to creating a better atmosphere in the Histadrut enterprises.

The setting up of a forum for joint deliberations on problems which formerly, before participation, were "out of bounds" for workers and their representatives has helped to avoid some of the tensions which used to arise as a result of having to accept "faits accomplis."

To sum up, it can be said that the managers no longer entrench themselves behind unjustified fears and apprehensions. Indeed, they sometimes make exaggerated demands on participation as though this were a magical formula which can be used from the moment it begins to function, to solve everything. They still must learn that participation opens a furrow, but that furrows must still be thoroughly and toilsomely ploughed. It takes a great deal of effort and time to change traditional attitudes in enterprises. The manager of the plant is the one who can ensure that the four above-mentioned criteria be followed in practice. He holds the keys for utilizing the potential of participation, and it depends mostly on him whether the reasonable prospects of success materialize. The question, in short, is whether the managers of plants look upon participation as a challenge for which it is worthwhile to endure psychological and organizational difficulties or rather as a nuisance.

There is no lack of obstacles. There is the fact that clear instructions regarding the methods of regular activities of Joint Managements sent to the plants by the Department of Participation and by the General Manager of the Industrial Concern "Koor" have not as yet led to adequate and smooth operation of all of them. The system of participative management should be learned by managers, as it is not just a new stage of negotiations between two sides, but much more than that—it is a new way of management itself.

Where the activities of Joint Managements follow the lines of our four criteria, the results are quite encouraging. The more faithfully those outlines are followed, the more promising are the returns. In any case, there is evidence that a growing number of managers already see the advantages and the positive prospects of participation.

What Is the Workers' Response?

Participation opens a new channel for labor relations. It provides a valuable tool for solving some of the problems which formerly were never even discussed in joint forum. How do the workers respond to the new opportunities to share in the process of decision-making at the plant afforded to them by participation?

As was to be expected, there is a wide spectrum of workers' attitudes towards participation, from complete rejection through indifference to various degrees of acceptance and to enthusiastic response. The reaction at the Histadrut economic enterprises to the fact that they employ hired labor "like everywhere else" is taking different forms—from total negation to the militant conclusion that "all should be changed" and the Histadrut economy should become "truly labor." The actual attitude depends on the level of education and labor-consciousness no less than on the local conditions. Nevertheless, the workers in dozens of plants voted in favor of participation, and this proves that it is possible to create an atmosphere necessary for a new joint venture, in sharing economic responsibility and in Industrial Democracy.

In the joint managements that have been set up, the workers' representatives display great interest in the problems of administration, complex management of enterprise finances, etc. In most cases they have proved to be good students and good partners, ready to learn, aware of the heavy responsibilities, and without inferiority complexes.

Still, workers do not automatically become converts to the idea, and —something no less important—to the practical duties of participation. It is easy to discern the difficulties which arise from the necessity to develop communication with fellow workers on new topics, or the need to report to the people on economic issues, current decisions of administrative and technical character, financial situation, etc. In this process some of the weaknesses of workers' organization in the plants make themselves felt.

The workers' committees are not accustomed to assembling the people for anything except election meetings or for some urgent needs, usually connected with bargaining for wages. Because there is quite a strain on committees, they avoid what they consider to be unnecessary gatherings without a defined purpose connected with their direct responsibilities. Lack of experience and insufficient knowledge make the members of these committees afraid that the tendency at every meeting will be to divert the discussions to the well-trodden questions of labor conditions and thus avoid other issues. This psychological attitude is disadvantageous to participation, which is based on regular, constant contact with the rank and file on all that is happening in the plants and in the various departments.

It is not altogether surprising that the Workers' Committees and Representatives in the plants must learn the art of constant communication with the rank and file. This is the essential part of participation—theory and practice—with a permanent flow of information and exchange of views and suggestions, upon which the whole system of workers' involvement stands or falls. Great efforts are made to persuade managers and workers alike of the necessity to break with the deeply rooted traditions in this respect. Yet there can be no mistake about the clear conclusions from accumulated evidence up to now. In order to surmount the reluctance toward closer and regular communication with the people on the "floor," two prior conditions are absolutely essential.

The first is to define fixed objectives for the plant, which should be presented by the Joint Management and discussed with the workers at all levels, each objective being supported by professional evidence, economic, technological, and organizational. It has been proved that in plants where this has been done at departmental and plant meetings, the deliberations were purposeful and also served as an outlet for people's initiative, understanding and self-esteem, contributing to the social spirit of the community. Meetings such as these require thorough preparations, but they assure genuine results. The other vital condition is participation in profits.

Profit-sharing schemes were previously, more often than not, a trick of the capitalist economic establishment. However, within the framework of a different approach, participation in profits may prove to be an important principle with economic and social effects. Participation in profits as an ingredient in full-scale participation in management and in the running of the undertaking makes it an entirely new concept. The success of this approach depends on close interrelation of both elements in participation. Profit-sharing, separated from organized and conscious involvement by the people, will deteriorate, sooner or later, into a paternalistic device of money grants from "Above."

On the other hand, participation in management divorced from any material returns will lack the all-important link with actual performance of the plant. There is no need to repeat once again that in general, and in participation in particular, there are things far more important than money—satisfaction in work, self-fulfillment, involvement, motivation, etc. Yet in a society where money is the measure of services and achievements, it is hard to assume that workers will make a long-term effort to accumulate profits for their plant if they do not share in them. At least this is the conclusion reached not only by theoretical analysis, but by practical experience. For this reason participation in profits is of vital importance.

"Koor," the largest Industrial Concern in the Labor Economy and roof organization of all Labor Enterprises, has chosen the straight way method of participation in the Balance-sheet profits of each plant, according to criteria approved by the Histadrut. For the past two years the workers in fifteen plants have received considerable amounts of money as their share in profits. As a beginning, this distribution of profits undoubtedly has had a very favorable influence on the feelings at the plants. Managers and workers alike reported enormous satisfaction following this proof of the changing status of workers in the Labor Economy.

All the same, we think that even the most imaginative schemes of profit-sharing will not advance workers' participation as a major development in our economy if it is not directly linked with the decision-making process. Passive waiting for the publication of the plant's Balance-sheet, usually more than a year after the commencement of the yearly work plan, cannot facilitate the use of profit-sharing as a tool of workers' involvement in the decisions made at the plant and their implementation. What is necessary from the point of view of workers' status in an enterprise is regular observation of the development of the plant as a whole and on departmental levels, joint deliberations and conclusions drawn at relatively brief intervals, with the purpose of implementing them, and a constant link between the joint management and the people on the production lines. Profit-sharing as an integral part of the participative management will contribute to the psychological effect of participation and at the same time bear economic results.

At the same plants there is experimentation with various programs of sharing the gains of efficiency, quality improvement, etc., which are conducted simultaneously with profit-sharing based on economic criteria.

It is too early to sum up the results of all these experiments, but up-to-date observation and analysis show that profit-sharing, if introduced as part of participation in management, adds to it an important positive element of "reality" and a concrete measure of achievements and failures.

LOOKING TO THE TASKS AHEAD

In these pages we have gone into the motives for workers' participation in the management of administrative labor economy, and described the efforts, and even struggles, for its implementation. However, it must be recalled once again that the complete picture of industrial democracy in our country contains the most glorious aspect of the workers' endeavors in Israel toward building a socialist society—the kibbutz movement and cooperation. This is the source of ideological strength which gives confidence that Labor Society (Hevrat Ovdim) is not only desirable but possible. This is where the drive to expand the boundaries of industrial democracy through the labor economy in order to bring them closer to the social model to which most of Israel's workers' strive comes from. The enormous experience gathered there will serve the beginnings in all sectors of the society because the workers' participation in management will not be limited to the labor economy alone.

There is no doubt whatsoever that workers' participation is appearing on the scene of national and private industry in Israel. The administrative sector of the labor economy directly belonging to the Histadrut must be the forerunner, but the experiment and the conclusions drawn from the labor enterprises will serve the entire society and the economy.

APPENDIX*
A few facts about the Histadrut:
* The Histadrut was founded in 1920. The entire membership at that time was 4433 workers.
* The membership of Histadrut in 1972 was 1,243,000 workers, employees, academicians, etc.
* 60,000 members are Arab and Druze.
* The population of Israel in 1972 was more than 3,250,000.
* The total number of employees in Israel in 1970 was 963,200; 709,200 of them are Histadrut members.
* By 1970 there were about 224,000 workers employed within the framework of Hevrat Ovdim. their total contribution to the National Net Product amounted to about 3.0 billion IL.
* Employment in Hevrat Ovdim industry rose from 37,400 workers in 1968 to 43,000 in 1970, representing an increase of 1%.

TABLE 1
Employees in Hevrat Obdim (Histadrut Enterprises)
and their Contribution to its Net Product, 1970

Division	Percentage of employees	Percentile Contri- bution to Net Product of Hevrat Ovdim
Cooperative Settlements— kibbutzim and moshavim	57	46
Wholly and partially owned enterprises	20	24
Histadrut non-profit institutions	10	10
Manufacturing, transportation and service cooperatives	8	11
Marketing and consumer associations	5	9

TABLE 2
Employment in Histadrut Enterprises as Compared
with National Economy, 1965-1970

Year	Histadrut	National Economy	Percentage of National Economy
1965	212,000	879,200	24.1%
1966	208,000	873,900	23.8%
1967	205,500	836,500	24.6%
1968	211,000	910,900	23.2%
1969	218,300	945,800	23.1%
1970	223,600	986,000	22.7%

TABLE 3
Employment in Histadrut Enterprises as Compared with the
National Economy, by Economic Branch (in percentages)

Economic Branch	1965	1966	1967	1968	1969	1970
Agriculture	70.0	72.5	74.0	75.2	75.7	78.0
Industry	15.5	14.5	19.5	15.5	15.8	16.0
Construction	23.0	25.2	26.7	24.9	26.0	26.5
Commerce, Banking and Finance	11.0	10.9	11.0	12.4	11.1	11.5
Transportation	26.1	26.8	25.0	23.7	22.2	19.7
Public Services	12.2	12.3	12.2	11.7	11.7	12.2
Personal Services	34.4	32.5	35.1	32.4	32.8	33.6
Total	24.1	23.8	23.6	23.2	23.1	22.7

This Table indicates that employment with Histadrut was on a relatively steady rise during the period in question, climbing from 70% to 78% of the labor force engaged in agriculture, and that construction saw a rise in relation to the national economy, increasing from 23% to 26.5% of the employees engaged in this sector of the Economy. Significantly, even during a period when industry within the national economy as a whole experienced great growth, Hevrat Ovdim held its own relative position in industry.

TABLE 4
Net Product of Hevrat Ovdim as Compared with the National Economy, Economic Branches (in percentages)

Economic Branches	1966	1967	1968	1969	1970
Agriculture	71.3	71.2	68.9	69.1	72.0
Industry	19.5	16.8	16.5	16.6	16.6
Construction	28.9	28.8	21.7	21.6	22.4
Commerce, Banking and Finance	14.8	15.3	14.5	14.3	14.9
Transportation	24.5	26.2	25.3	22.7	20.3
Public Services	11.2	11.0	10.7	10.6	10.3
Personal Services	22.9	22.9	20.4	19.2	10.9
Total	21.4	21.1	20.0	19.5	19.0

TABLE 5
Net Product of the Hevrat Ovdim Economy as Compared with the National Economy, 1965-1970 (at current prices)

Year	Hevrat Ovdim	National Economy	Percentage of National Economy
	(IL Mil.)	(IL Mil.)	
1965	1,928.0	8,570.2	22.5
1966	2,031.6	9,423.0	21.4
1967	2,070.0	9,798.5	21.1
1968	2,325.0	11,632.0	20.8
1969	2,573.0	13,176.0	19.5
1970	2,964.0	15,200.0	19.5
1971	3,400.0	16,800.0	20.0

There is also a very impressive growth in tourism, in organizations serving industry, in financial institutions and in services such as those offered by the Alda export company.

TABLE 6
Employment in Hevrat Ovdim Industry, by Branches, 1968-1970

Industrial Branch	Number of Employees			Percent of Total			Rate of Growth		
	1968	1969	1970	1968 %	1969 %	1970 %	1969/68 %	1970/69 %	
Food Industry	15,300	15,800	15,800	41	38	36	103	100	
Metal and Machinery	7,300	8,000	9,000	20	21	21	110	112	
Electrical and Electronic Equipment	3,100	4,100	4,900	9	10	12	132	119	
Leather, Rubber and Plastic	1,700	2,000	2,100	4	5	5	117	105	
Oil, Chemicals and Pharmaceuticals	700	900	1,100	1	2	3	128	122	
Quarries, Cement and Ceramics	3,000	3,100	3,200	8	8	9	103	103	
Wood and Paper	3,800	3,900	3,900	10	9	8	102	100	
Printing and Publishing	700	800	800	2	2	1	114	100	
Textiles and Clothing	1,300	1,200	1,300	4	3	3	92	108	
Miscellaneous Manufacturing	500	800	900	1	2	2	160	112	
Total	37,400	40,600	43,000	100	100	100	108	106	

NOTES

1. The Hisatdrut with affiliated Labor Economy is simultaneously the Trade-Union Movement in Israel, with 85 percent of all workers in the country organized in its ranks.

*Figures and Tables are taken from "Hevrat Ovdim in the Israeli Economy", 1972.

7

INDUSTRIAL DEMOCRACY IN NORWAY: EMPLOYEE REPRESENTATION AND PERSONAL PARTICIPATION

by Einar Thorsrud
Senior Research Fellow, World Research Institute, Oslo.
and Fred E. Emery
Senior Research Fellow, Research School of Social Science,
Australian National University, Canberra

THE Industrial Democracy Program in Norway has the following characteristics as a research strategy. First, it grew out of a widespread public discussion of alienation in industry and the utilization of human resources. This led to a research activity jointly sponsored by unions and employers' organizations and later by government. Secondly, over a period of eight years, social scientists from three institutes in two different countries have been able to cooperate actively with the sponsors on company, branch, and national levels. Thirdly, each phase of the research program was evaluated by the sponsors as to the relevance of the findings to what they felt were the important problems. Then the next phase was planned accordingly. While the first phase had been concerned with the representation of employees on company boards, the second phase provided for four field experiments to change the conditions for personal participation in actual work situations. In this article we shall present our major ideas and conclusions regarding employee representation and then we will outline an alternative approach to problems of industrial democracy.

THE CONCEPT OF INDUSTRIAL DEMOCRACY IN NORWAY

Like most concepts that lead men to action, "industrial democracy" has a hierarchy of meanings. At a very general level, there would probably be wide agreement with the dictionary definition that industrial democracy means distribution of social power in industry among all who are engaged in the work rather than its concentration in the hands of a minority. This level of agreement is certainly not so general as to be meaningless. Power concentrated in the hands of a minority, even though it may make a great deal of difference to the majority whether this power is exercised justly and with due consideration for their interests would not, strictly speaking, exemplify the notion of industrial democracy.

General agreement about democracy, and hence about industrial democracy, is not limited to the definition and correct usage of the term. Among those who specialize in the study of institutions, there is a large consensus with regard to the social conditions which are necessary in practice for a democratic distribution of social power. Quite briefly, these conditions are:

1) That men are assumed to be equal human beings. If, on the contrary, some are assumed to be of inferior caste or to be second-rate, then despite any formal arrangements they will tend to be deprived of effective representation.

2) That all men have such freedom of movement in their daily lives that they may, if they desire, make an autonomous contribution to the life of the community. If, on the contrary, men are extremely restricted by the need to earn a living, by censorship, or in other ways, then no formal arrangements for representation will create an effective democracy.

3) That the leadership is removable by, and responsible to, the many. If the available leadership is, on the contrary, controlled by some political party or machine, or loyal to a narrow social stratum, then elections and the like will not ensure effective democracy.

It is easy to see why, in recent decades, political scientists have had to spell out the differences between real and apparent democracy, and it is clear that parallel distinctions need to be borne in mind in considering industrial democracy.

However, the point of special relevance to our purposes is that general agreement disappears whenever people attempt to make industrial democracy a meaningful concept in a particular social setting.

The first wave of discussions and political actions related to industrial democracy appeared in Norway, as it did in some other countries, at the time of the First World War. Under the pressure of industrial unrest, a law was passed to establish work councils in industrial companies. The councils were supposed to deal with matters of joint interest to both labor and management. The law was never really implemented although it did exist for more than thirty years. The representatives of labor soon realized that they achieved much more through national agreements established between unions and management organizations. The first of these agreements, reached in 1935, is still looked upon as the Magna Charta of industry. After the Second World War they were extended to cover not only the rights of workers to organize and bargain for wages and work conditions, but also to be informed and consulted in major company affairs.

The concept of industrial democracy always has political overtones.

This was the case also in Norway in the early 1960's, although the concept meant something more than *workers' control and employee representation.* In conjunction with their major role in collective bargaining and the maintenance of industrial peace, the main organizations in Norway have experience with all aspects of joint consultation on the company level, a well-established part of the Scandinavian system of industrial relations. On the other hand, the results of workers' councils, production committees, suggestion systems, etc., were not impressive.

The placing of representatives of employees directly onto the boards of companies might seem to be a very simple way to open radically new possibilities in terms of industrial democracy. Some state-owned companies introduced such schemes around 1950. Trade union leaders in Norway were not prepared to act directly on this development. Nor were they in a position to evaluate similar experiences abroad. They turned to a group of social scientists for help. It was felt that whatever the scientists had to offer would be seriously considered by those who should take social and political responsibility. To be able to formulate a research program, it was necessary first to define industrial democracy in the Norwegian setting. An analysis of statements by leaders in politics, trade unions, and business and interviews with them helped to clarify the issue.

(1) It was clearly recognized that industrial democracy must be considered in the context of existing Norwegian industrial conditions based on a set of broad, but practical and reliable agreements on labor-management cooperation, arbitration, and conciliation, and the effects of income policies on national productivity.

(2) In considering the purposes of industrial democracy there was no apparent willingness to sacrifice what had already been achieved in living conditions or labor relations. At the same time, however, there was a generally shared feeling that steps towards industrial democracy should be taken in order to (a) bring Norwegian industrial life into closer accord with the democratic social life that individuals now enjoy, and to (b) create the conditions of fuller individual commitment that will lead to increased productivity and efficiency.

There was no indication that people believed that both goals must be met together although there was some suggestion that it would not be acceptable for one to be achieved at the expense of the other.

(3) There was a general uncertainty with regard to the organizational forms that would enhance democracy in industry. Different spokesmen referred to the shortcomings of different schemes for formal representation of the employees and there appeared to be a common belief that industrial democracy in Norway must mean something more than just formal democratic arrangements of elections, representation, decisions by committee, etc.

(4) From several quarters came the suggestion that this "something more" pertained to the conditions under which individuals carry out their ordinary day-to-day tasks in the workplace, i.e., something akin to what the specialists identify as the necessary conditions or requirements of democracy.

THE EFFECTS OF EMPLOYEE REPRESENTATION ON COMPANY BOARDS

Based on analysis of different representative systems in Yugoslavia, West Germany, and Great Britain, the social scientists proceeded with a study of five companies in Norway. All these companies had more than ten years of experience with employee representation at board level. To limit the danger of overgeneralizing from the evidence, three points must be borne in mind with respect to the representatives interviewed. First, the five companies were, by Norwegian standards, large manufacturing firms, which were all wholly or in part financed by state capital. One could expect the situation here to be more favorable to the experiment than would have been the case in private companies in Norway. Second, the representatives had accepted a personal commitment to their role which might have led to a tendency to overestimate their own achievements. Third, some thirty people who had had personal experience on these boards were interviewed. Twelve out of these had acted as representatives, the others in key roles as Chairmen or Managing Directors.

Apart from simply reasserting that representation on the boards implemented the employees' right to be heard (i.e., that it increased democracy) the interviewees indicated several specific purposes that could be served by representation:

1) It could serve as a control on the way management carried out its personnel functions.

2) It could discourage the Board from considering measures that would be very unpopular with the employees.

3) It could increase the chances of the Board's making decisions taking into account the interests of their employees. Thus an employees' representative could help to draw the Board's attention to the need for investment in welfare (housing, pensions, etc.).

These are possibilities and by no means all of the representatives thought they had realized all of them. One should indeed ask "how effective are these influences" and "how far do they contribute to the intended aims of democratization? How does their effectiveness compare with that of alternative means?"

Several relevant facts emerged from the interviews. First, there is little evidence of active communication and feedback between the electors and their representative. This in itself casts some doubt on the effectiveness of the representation, particularly since the representatives' mandate is rather short. Furthermore, nine out of the twelve representatives interviewed made some reference to their having to take a board or company view of some matters, particularly production. These facts concur with those resulting from the other interviews (with Chairmen and Managing Directors) and with the records of Board meetings. Together they suggest that it may not be easy in practice for representatives to exercise control over the managers in personnel matters, to restrain the board, or to push welfare demands too hard in the face of other company requirements that they may be ill-equipped to judge.

A detailed analysis of analogous experience in Yugoslavia, Germany, and Great Britain confirmed the general picture.

The Norwegian case studies bring into sharper focus some of the issues that emerged from the foreign experience. In particular, there is the distinction between negotiating and reconciling between different but related sources of power (as, for instance, trade unions exercise their power in negotiations for the interests of employees) and matters that seem to involve sharing of power. A necessary condition for the continued sharing of power is that there must be agreement on means and goals that are mutually compatible. If, in the extreme case, power is used for contradictory and mutually defeating purposes, then the basis for sharing will almost certainly be disrupted. Effective sharing does of course require more than the absence of contradictory ends or means; it requires that the various ends and means be mutually supportive. Moreover, if sharing of any source of social power is not to be disruptive of other parts of society, then it must go hand in hand with the sharing of responsibility. Looking at the behavior of employee representatives on Norwegian boards, it becomes clear that although they legally share in the power of the Board, they find it very difficult to see how to use this power in ways that are in accord with the usual Board purposes, and at the same time have a direct impact on the working life of their constituents. The power of the Board relates to and is appropriately used for the economic prosperity of the firm. Most of the known and obvious ways of furthering the employees' interests at Board level involve an increase in labor costs, with no assurance of an offsetting economic gain for the company, or they involve interference in managerial execution of Board policy which a Board member will be naturally reluctant to advocate. The possibilities for jointly furthering the interests of the employees and the company seem to be more in the sphere of the manager than at the Board level. As a consequence, the employees' representatives find themselves in a position where they can do only one of the following:

1) Work along with the rest of the Board, in the hope that increased prosperity for the firm will result in greater job security and increased rewards for the employees. In this way there can be a genuine sharing in the power of the Board, but this is at a personal level and does not depend on there being representatives of the employees. The responsibility they assume when they act in this way is a responsibility to the Board.

2) Act as members of the Board who happen to have some information about the temper of the workers, etc., which might help them decide on their strategies. If, however, they decide to act in their role as employees' representatives then they will find themselves negotiating against the interests represented by the rest of the Board. This could not be pushed far without involving, explicitly or implicitly, the power of the employees vis-a-vis the company.

Thus the introduction of a workers' representative onto the board takes place in such a way that he finds himself under pressure to become a "regular" board member. He cannot at the same time be a trade union official. Nor is he allowed to take up personnel problems of particular employees. Such problems are referred to the personnel department or to the managers.

All the board members were agreed on these principles, and the representatives generally observed them. They did not always find it easy to do so, and this was understood and appreciated by other board members. When conflict situations arose between the company and its employees or their union, it seemed to be *not* as board members but as trade unionists that the representatives had their difficulties.

Several references were made in interviews to occasions when representatives had been told explicitly that some board problem would have to be discussed without their presence. On other occasions the representative was present, but realized quite clearly that he could not take part in certain decisions; and in yet other instances he had been told explicitly that he could not participate in discussion or decision-making but that he could be present because the board relied on him not to pass information to anyone outside. This did not happen only to representatives of workers or staff. The same principle was applied to board members who held a position in an organization that was selling or buying from the company.

On balance it is easier for the workers' representative to avoid playing this role on the board than to play it. His constituents seem less active in pressing for allegiance than the other board members in pressing for allegiance to the board. Thus, there is evidence that the workers' representatives generally changed their outlook and assumed that of the board members and they found participation easier the further they developed this outlook.[3]

Because the balance of forces favors them, the other board members usually find that they can keep representatives' activities on behalf of outside interest groups to a tolerable minimum. This they do by excluding negotiation, and by discouraging or ruling out-of-order any efforts to bring up problems of individual workers or matters relating to the personnel function of management—or at least by minimizing the leakage of relevant information to outside bodies.

If we were to summarize the results of the study of this particular democracy it would be as follows:

(1) There seems to be a case for extending the area of negotiations within the firm. Work Councils and the like are potentially capable of handling a large number of problems as they arise in their concrete work setting. These problems might otherwise remain unresolved and create bad relations, or they might be translated into some other, more difficult problem so that they can be handled by the existing trade union organizations. The general experience is that these benefits of representational systems can be realized only if they are matched by an effective management.

In general the management must recognize that the success of their enterprise depends upon how it works as a sociotechnical system, not simply as a technical system with replaceable individuals added to it. In particular, management needs to have a personnel system that keeps them informed of the condition of their employees and makes it possible for management to exercise some initiative in the matter, and thus demonstrate their sincerity and goodwill. Furthermore, management requires an effective appeals system. Without this, the work of the representative (and negotiating) system will be too easily disturbed and distorted by individual cases.

(2) Insofar as industrial democracy means more than extended negotiations and consultations, there is need for some transfer of real managerial power to the employees. It is difficult indeed to see how this sharing can be started at the top—at Board level. If democratic participation is to be a reality then it seems inevitable that this must be started at a level where a large proportion of employees are *both* able and willing to participate. The problem of creating industrial democracy seems in fact to be inseparable from the problem of the split at the bottom of the executive apparatus which has plagued all attempts to create effective representational systems. Fortunately, this latter does not seem to be an insoluble problem. Holter's (1965) survey of the attitude of Norwegian workers confirms the findings in other comparable democratic societies that the majority of the lower grades of industrial workers feel that they (a) could cope with more responsibility in their daily work, and (b) want more such responsibility. Industrial experiments in the United States, Great Britain, and India (in engineering, coal mining, and textiles) have shown that democratic sharing of managerial power at this level can be stable and effective because it furthers the ends of both employees and management. (Trist 1963, Tannenbaum 1966).

AN ALTERNATIVE APPROACH TO INDUSTRIAL DEMOCRACY

The report on Phase A (worker representation on Boards) of the Industrial Democracy Program as presented above was discussed widely in Norway when it appeared in 1964. Drafts of the report had already been discussed and evaluated by the representatives of the major labor and management organizations. Trade Unions as well as the Confederation of Employers published their own policies on industrial democracy. The joint research committee agreed with the social scientists that a second phase of research should concentrate on conditions for personal participation.

On existing evidence, it appeared that the manner in which employees participate in the work-life of their companies is critical for the use they make of formal mechanisms for representation and consultation, and also for their attitudes of apathy or constructive interest, of dissatisfaction or satisfaction.

The bulk of the scientific evidence suggested that the more the individual is enabled to exercise control over his task, and to relate his efforts to those of his fellows, the more likely is he to accept a positive commitment. This positive commitment shows in a number of ways, not the least of which is the release of that personal initiative and creativity which constitute the basis of a democratic climate.

However, there is no simple technique that can be applied in all industrial conditions to bring about these changes. Thus, while job enlargement has proved effective in some conditions, it would be inappropriate in others; the development of autonomous work groups has been effective in some conditions, but likewise would be ineffective in others; in some cases increased skills may be essential, but in others no such changes may be called for. The important point is that the kinds of change required are likely to be related to the kind of technology involved.

Some basic hypotheses for job design and organizational development were developed for testing in real work situations. We shall only mention the general psychological requirements implicit in these hypotheses:

(1) the need for the content of a job to be reasonably demanding of the worker in terms other than sheer endurance, and yet to provide a minimum of variety (not necessarily novelty);

(2) the need for being able to learn on the job and to go on learning; this again is a question of neither too much nor too little;

(3) the need for some minimal area of decision-making that the individual can call his own;

(4) the need for some minimal degree of social support and recognition in the workplace;

(5) the need for the individual to be able to relate what he does and what he produces to his social life;

(6) the need to feel that the job leads to some sort of desirable future.

These requirements are not confined to operators on the factory floor, nor is it possible to meet them in the same way in all work settings or for all kinds of people.

For five years we (the authors) have conducted four extensive field experiments in different companies. It is most relevant to report in this context the research strategy used. It will illustrate an alternative approach to industrial democracy. We shall list the major steps in our strategy.

(1) *Establishment of a Joint Committee* representing labor and management was the first step taken in 1962 (before Phase A started). This body was designed to assist the researchers in planning, initiating, carrying out, and evaluating the research. The joint committee proved to be of particular importance in the initiation and evaluation phases. Also at certain critical points of change the joint committee played an active and important role. One aspect of this role was the support it gave to the managers and local union officials who had to accept the responsibility for experimental changes in their plants. Another aspect was the assurance given by its continued presence as an appeal body and a potential source of sanctions in those cases where major issues were best dealt with at a higher level than that of the organization involved in the field experiment.

(2) *The choice of an experimental company* was made in collaboration with the joint committee mentioned above and the management and union inside the company. The choice was made on the basis of criteria set up by the researchers and agreed to by the committee. The main criteria were: type of technology and product, the position of the company in the branch, the geographic location of the company, and the level of labor-management relations inside the firm. These were thought to affect the relevance, potential influence, and the possibility of successful change.

(3) *A systematic analysis* of each selected company was made in order to get a general outline of critical variations in the relations of the company (as a system) to its environment; we analyzed its product markets, input of raw materials, contact with technological developments in research and education, the financial situation, marketing relations, and finally the labor market and other links to community institutions. The companies assisted with these analyses. This research took us beyond the question of "willingness to change" to the question of ability to tolerate extended experimental changes in the face of environmental demands and pressures.

(4) *Choice of experimental sites* within the companies was made in collaboration with management and the shop stewards of the plant. The choice was influenced by the kind of technology involved, the strategic position of the department inside the company, and the attitude of management and employees toward experimenting along the lines of our research. As far as possible we wanted a site with a fairly clearly defined boundary but also well placed, strategically, for subsequent diffusion of the results. This meant that improvements in the control of variation inside one department could be readily perceived as advantageous for the preceding and subsequent phases of production. This would be likely to induce those responsible to try to achieve similar changes in their own departments.

(5) *Establishing action committees* with representatives of operators, supervisors, and factory and departmental management proved to be crucial for the continuance of the field experiments. In the beginning of the experiments the research group was very active but gradually the action committees had to assume full responsibility for the carrying out of the research project inside the company. This appeared to be a prerequisite for the involvement of the operators.

(6) *Sociotechnical analysis of the experimental sites* was undertaken in cooperation with the action group and company specialists. The major steps in the sociotechnical analysis can be summarized as follows:

(a) The analysis starts with a description of the variations in inputs and outputs of the department and measurements of the significant sources of variation in quality and quantity during the transformation of inputs. Estimates are made also of departmental capabilities. For example, measurements include variations in services, technical equipment, personnel, and management.

(b) Drawing upon the experience of operators, management, and specialists, we try to assess the relative importance of different variations which have been registered during the first step. Usually a matrix can be constructed that shows the relations between the different kinds of variation. This is the most effective way of identifying cases of task interdependence which are not reflected in the current structuring of responsibilities and power or which require technical changes. These matrices are also valuable in identifying production subsystems and in identifying the criteria actually used for judging the importance of critical variation. These criteria operationally define the primary task of the department and make it possible to set up an effective system for feedback of results.

(c) A description is made of the formal organization in terms of positions, work roles, recruitment, and training.

(d) Analysis is made of the communication network, partly through interviews, partly through observations, and partly through analysis of record flows. The aim is to construct a conceptual model of the network and to test it against various independent sources of evidence.

(e) Systematic interviews are conducted with personnel to get a baseline measure of satisfactions and dissatisfactions with the old system. The attitude survey is usually structured around the basic psychological job requirements. In this way we have a chance to measure what improvements of conditions for personal participation actually take place.

(f) Analysis is made of wage and salary system to see how well it reflects current distributions of effort and responsibility. If they are properly matched, this is a major inducement to greater personal participation.

(7) *The company policy* usually has to be described in concrete terms with respect to such management practices as job allocation, training and job incentives, and also with respect to product markets for raw materials, "know-how," labor, capital, and products. In defining company policy, we have found it necessary to identify how and by whom policy is made because experimentation in generating units involves questions of company policy.

(8) *Program for change* is drafted in cooperation with the personnel of the chosen department and the company specialists. The action group plays a major role in formulating and presenting the program for change. Typical features of a change program are:

(a) Multiskilling of operators so that they can alternate between different work roles inside partly autonomous groups. This departs from the prevalent philosophy of "one man—one skill."

(b) Development of the measures of variation and of the data-analysis methods needed for control has been traditionally held at a level too remote for quick and detailed control action and hence it did not need the requisite information. In one case the establishment of a new information room was a major part during one phase of an experiment.

(c) Attachment of a local repairman to back up the quick and detailed control actions for which the operators are expected to assume responsibility.

(d) Institutionalizing the meetings, contacts, etc., that enable the operators, as a group, to plan and coordinate their activities.

(e) Training the foreman to supervise, coordinate, and plan for the activities of groups rather than individuals. This usually means an extension of their time-span of responsibility and some skilling in tasks of appraisal, diagnosis, and planning of production which are traditionally located at middle management level.

(f) Design and introduction of new bonus arrangement if the department has or needs some special kind of incentive schemes. The analysis of variation in terms of quantity and quality will usually have been done during previous phases of analysis and can now be applied as a basis for an incentive to work and learn as a group with regard to a wide spectrum of departmental objectives.

(9) *Institutionalization of a continued learning and organizational change process* is the final stage of the development project. Gradually the change process, and the responsibility for it, must shift from the action committee to the management and shop stewards or be otherwise assigned to formal parts of the work organization in terms of standing committees, etc. This can only be accomplished by embodying the lessons of the experiment in the philosophy or style of management through appropriate organizational changes.

(10) *Diffusion of results* has been an objective of all the experimental companies, that is, that they would carry a certain responsibility for publicizing research inside the branch and the industry as such. The central joint committee took a major responsibility for the diffusion process, together with the researchers, but it was obviously going to be necessary for the experimental plants to act as demonstration sites. Gradually the researchers would have to take less responsibility for the diffusion of results and concentrate mainly on reanalysis and reformulation of the hypothesis and principles that formed the basis of these experiments.

Most of the above steps were necessary in the four experiments we have run so far as part of the Industrial Democracy Project. Rather than looking at each of these steps as part of a cookbook recipe, one should look at each step as a condition for change; sometimes the sequence will change and sometimes a shop will have to be adapted to the particular situation in the company or experimental departments.

The steps can all be summarized as four basic aspects of change, namely:
(1) *Information*
(2) *Involvement*
(3) *Commitment*
(4) *Actual social change.*

CONCLUDING REMARKS

It is too early to make a final evaluation of the results of these experiments from a social science point of view;[4] however, the results are encouraging since a number of new experiments are spreading in Norwegian and Swedish industry under the sponsorship of joint Trade Union and Management committees. Several European study groups have come to visit the field sites.

In the wake of this development in industry a wide range of new research problems and possibilities are facing the social scientists. Apart from the follow-up studies, experiments with new roles of supervisors seem to be important. Alternative forms of specialist roles and production management are emerging. Trade Unions have also started to question their own organizational patterns. On board ships, experiments with multipurpose crews lead to studies of flexible career systems and new educational arrangements. So far we have been hesitant to enter the educational field. But it seems quite obvious by now that we ought to do more than to speculate as to the next steps if the industrial projects really take root. The effects on education are perhaps easiest to surmise because we are already involved in education of managers and others for roles in the new sociotechnical systems. On the basis of educational changes following the industrial experiments we have also become involved in development of new strategies of change in general education.

NOTES

1. Permission to quote from a book by the same authors, *Form and Content in Industrial Democracy,* is given by Tavistock Publications.

2. This particular formulation is derived from Karl Mannheim's "Essays on the Sociology of Culture," 1956, pp. 177-179.

3. This kind of role conflict has received a lot of attention from social scientists. The position of the employee representative can be represented as in (a) below. Such a structure is inherently unstable (see Heider, 1959). By attenuating his trade union relation (b) the representative gets out of this double bind. The other solution would be to fight the board.

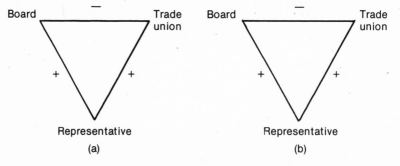

4. The report on the four field experiments in industrial companies was published in Norway in 1970. (Thorsrud E. and Emery F. E. *Mot en ny bedrifts-organisasjon.* Tanum, Oslo: 1970). English edition to appear 1973.

REFERENCES

Emery, F. E. and Thorsrud, E. *Form and Content in Industrial Democracy.* London: Tavistock, 1969. (Distributed in United States by Barnes & Noble, Inc.)

Heider, F. *The Psychology of Interpersonal Relations.* New York: Wiley, 1959.

Holter, H. "Attitudes towards Employee Participation in Company Decision Making." *Human Relations,* Vol. 18, 1965, pp. 297-321.

Mannheim, K. *Essays on the Sociology of Culture.* London: Oxford University Press, 1956.

Tannenbaum, A. S. *Social Psychology of the Work Organization.* Belmont, Calif., 1966.
Thorsrud E. and Emery, F. E. Mot en ny bedril
Trist, E. et al. *Organizational Choice.* London: Tavistock, 1963.

Edited Excerpts from the
DIALOGUE
held at the
Center for the Study of Democratic Institutions,
Santa Barbara, California, October 1971

NAMES OF PARTICIPANTS IN THE *DIALOGUE*
(as they occur)

ANDERSON, ARTHUR G.	THORSRUD, EINAR
BORGESE, ELISABETH	ASHMORE, HARRY S.
MANN	PARDO, ARVID
McWHINNEY, WILLIAM	PACEK, JOZE
ADIZES, ICHAK	WHEELER, HARVEY
PASIC, NAJDAN	McCOY, PRESSLEY
NEAL, FRED WARNER	ECHEVERRIA, MANUEL
BRUCAN, SILVIU	ROCK, WILLIAM P.

WHY SELF-MANAGEMENT?

ANDERSON: Most of us are aware of the need for change. As more people attain higher levels of education, jobs which provide no personal satisfaction or no personal development become increasingly unacceptable. This applies also to the educational institutions themselves where people are demanding a role in the layout of their own work; and it applies to a great number of other institutions. (I restrict my observations to the situation in the developed countries, using the United States as an example.)

I was introduced to the subject of self-management in my own sphere of activity, which is industrial research. In a research organization it is impossible to tell people what to do in detail. People must be able to plan the organization of their own work, or participate in the planning and layout.

One of the aims of this conference is to explore how people, in general, could become more involved, could gain control over their own work and derive a sense of personal development and learning from their work.

BORGESE: The theory of self-management implies a postindustrial ideology. It implies an ideology for a learning society and for a society that has to face constant change. It is a philosophy that is not dualistic, that overcomes the dichotomy between individual and society, a philosophy in which self-fulfillment and social fulfillment tend to coincide.

It provides an alternative to the structure of the corporation, the big multinational corporation which so often is being celebrated as a new "model" for international organization but in reality represents just another form of a closed and hierarchical structure.

Self-management provides a structure that straddles the economic order, the social order, and the political order. And I think that this is the kind of structure to which the future belongs. At the international level, organizations like the European Economic Communities, or organizations like the ocean regime on which we have been working, have these same characteristics. There is no longer any separation between the economic, the social, and the political. Self-management therefore is applicable not only to economic organizations but to territorial organizations as well. It is applicable to nationalities, to minorities, to universities.

Self-management theory, furthermore, provides an adequate organizational structure for the new concept of social ownership, or rather nonownership, that is developing all over the world and of which the "common heritage of mankind" concept in the oceans is a first tangible example. If the world community adopts as a basis for its organization this concept of the "common heritage of mankind," which is the same thing as social property (which means nonproperty) then I think the experiment in self-management and its structuralization in a participatory system, the self-management system, has enormous lessons for all of us today.

McWHINNEY: Self-management implies much more than industrial decision-making. It develops techniques which lead to self-potentiation and self-realization not only in industrial life or work life, but also in political life, in personal life, and in the community in general. So, if we have created a self-managing society, that means we have created individuals who have the personal ability to participate, as opposed to withdrawing into the alienated behavior that is so typical of most of our modern industrial society.

ADIZES: I believe that the Yugoslav system as it is now operating, with the experience that has accumulated in twenty years, has something to offer to the rest of the world because it is a structure that has enabled rapid change in the political, social, and technological environment. Any organization, any structure that has made possible such a rate of change, I think, should be studied in depth.

Self- or community-management as a vehicle for effective decentralization is something the Yugoslavs have experienced, and something from which we in the United States can learn. In the turbulent United States environment there is an increasing need for regulation of the interactions, overlapping interests, and confluences deriving from the intensity of the environment. I would say that there is a strong trend toward recentralization, passing the regulating rights to an existing institution which already has power, i.e., the government. The self-management system is a vehicle to retard this recentralization process. For self-management in the microcommunity of work cannot survive if the macrocommunity of the State remains centralized and hierarchical.

So, whenever we talk about self-management, the political implication is retardation of centralization, something which is of great value for developed nations. Additionally, the postindustrial society needs organizational structures that will satisfy the growing need for self-realization and personal growth.

In the developing nations, on the other hand, self-management serves yet other purposes. It enhances the willingness to sacrifice, which is essential for rapid capital formation. It also enhances willingness to endure the stress inherent in the process of industrialization.

Self-management was introduced in Yugoslavia when it was still largely an underdeveloped agricultural country with a high rate of illiteracy. In the opinion of many theorists, an industrial system based on workers' participation is premature in such a situation. Self-management in Yugoslavia, however, turned out to be beneficial in two ways. First, it created a system that required the workers to study, learn, and develop in order to operate in it. The alienating effects of the process of industrialization could be minimized via the process of participation in decision-making and rewards. Self-management created the need for education and at the same time enabled this education process to take place, thus offering a sense of psychological security to a society under the stress of industrialization.

Second, self-management hastened the process of economic development. In a community where workers feel that they are working for themselves, togetherness induces a higher level of sacrifice. In a hierarchical structure, with orders coming from the top, workers will question the need for greater sacrifice and harder work—especially under conditions where there is a lack of correlation between results and efforts. The imposition of sacrifice can generate a backlash against management and the system itself. Self-management enhances the spirit of sacrifice, and this has enabled the Yugoslav system to pass through the turbulent change from central planning to decentralization, from an agricultural to an industrialized society.

The same phenomenon can be observed in other developing countries, such as Peru. Workers, even though still illiterate, will work harder when they realize that they are part of the system, that they are not working for some distant unknown owner or ruler, but for themselves.

THE YUGOSLAV EXPERIENCE

PASIC: The postwar development of Yugoslavia has attracted wide international attention which is not in proportion to the size of the country and its economic and military strength. This attention is due, in my opinion, primarily to the fact that Yugoslavia has developed a system of self-management. There are many people in the world today who are sincerely worried and alarmed about the tendency toward large-scale bureaucratization in politics and in social affairs. These people accept the scientific diagnosis of Max Weber and Robert Mitchell. They recognize the validity of the gloomy artistic forecasts of Orville, Huxley, and Kafka. Self-management may offer a historical alternative to the trend of bureaucratization, an alternative for many millions of people who today are helpless in the face of huge bureaucratic organizations which determine the conditions of their life. Self-management raises the hope of regaining the necessary degree of economic and political and moral autonomy.

While Yugoslavia obviously has not provided the world with a fully developed and perfect ideal model of self-management, the fact is that it is the only country in the contemporary world that has made a deliberate, genuine, and large-scale effort to transfer the ideas of self-management from the sphere of theory into the sphere of political and social action. Both achievements and failures in Yugoslavia are therefore relevant for those who are interested in self-management, who want to learn something about it and judge its values.

The Concept and the Mechanism

In building our self-management system in Yugoslavia, we have not been by far so pragmatic or dogmatic as we are sometimes blamed (or praised) for. Let me mention quite briefly some of the fundamental ideas underlying the general concept of self-management as it developed in Yugoslavia since the early fifties.

The first and most important idea is that of the emancipation and liberation of labor. This is a Marxist idea which we think to be, as a matter of fact, the humanistic essence of socialist transformation. To achieve this goal it is necessary to abolish relationships of exploitation in all their forms. Only if the worker obtains effective control over means, conditions, and results of his work, will he be able to control the social forces which are produced by his own collective work. He will be able to control the immediate direct political power in the society. The way to achieve such liberation is the transformation of state ownership into public social ownership, or nonproperty, under the direct control of associated labor.

Every socialist society in which private property was abolished has been faced with a crucial dilemma, and that is the question: to whom will belong that enormous social, political, and economic power accruing from the management of publicly owned means of production? Will that enormous power belong to a state bureaucracy or to the working people themselves? The importance of self-management in our view is that it solves that crucial problem in favor of workingmen. So by developing self-management we overcome the situation in which government is the universal owner and universal manager of the whole economy, which always implies the danger that this enormous power might be transformed into political oppression. By transforming state ownership into public ownership under the control of the workers themselves, we deprive bureaucracy of the main source of its power. In Yugoslavia we have tried to apply simple principles: that he who works also manages. In other words, work with the publicly owned means of production will be organized only on the principle of self-management. That is a constitutional principle with us.

Self-managed enterprises are autonomous commodity producers for the market. So we try—and I hope we have succeeded to some extent—to solve the problem of compatibility of public ownership and market economy. This means the restoration of a vital connection between production and consumption since the driving force in the development of the society and the expansion of productive forces is not compulsion of the workers from above but their own economic interests. This has, of course, a great effect on the rise of productivity and on the dynamism of the whole economic system.

Every unit of work, every institution has been turned into a school of democratic and political socialization because people can learn in their daily practice the close interconnection between their personal achievements and the success of the enterprise to which they belong and which they manage.

These changes have also facilitated the consistent implementation of the principle of national equality which is of great importance for a country such as Yugoslavia. The same principle of self-management—that every individual and group should control the income it creates—is applied also in the relationship among nations. This provides the basis for better mutual understanding and for the realization of the principle of national freedom and equality in a multinational country like Yugoslavia.

The second basic idea I should mention just briefly is that we have made of self-management a general pattern of social organization.

Gradually self-management has been extended to other fields of social life, not only in the economy, but in public services such as education, health service, social insurance, and so on. Every school, every hospital in Yugoslavia is a self-managed institution in which the working people have almost the same position and the same rights to self-management as their fellow workers in the factories. And this, in our view, is the basis for overcoming the contradictions between manual and intellectual labor, the difference between the economic-material sphere of life and other fields of human activity.

The third basic idea is the transformation of the system of general political representation by introducing new forms of direct democracy. Self-management, in our view, implies more than decentralization in the economy and other spheres of life. It requires the abolishment of hierarchical structures in every single cell, in every working unit, in every institution of the society. This principle generates a revolutionary change in the pattern of interest articulation. It offers the possibility for direct expression of individual and personal interest at every level of social organization. In that way the ground is prepared for a revival of direct democracy and for the development of new forms of direct democratic confrontations of different interests. The importance of those political organizations which mediate between the citizen and the authorities or the political decision-making centers has been reduced. In that way also, the role of the Communist Party in Yugoslavia has been basically changed and democratized. It is no longer so much the dominating force in a one-party system as it used to be.

Thus, instead of general political representatives, we have in the Yugoslav Assembly more and more nonprofessional deputies who remain on their working posts and who really channel the impulses from the working organizations into those centers of political decision-making.

Lytton Strachey in his book *New Capitalism* said at one point that parliamentary democracy should be judged not only by what it gives but by what it prevents. I think the same criterion should be applied when we evaluate the merits and the failings of self-management, not only by what it gives but also by what it prevents, e.g., the tendency of bureaucratization and technocratic oppressiveness of modern society.

It is our conviction that people should not have self-management only in their work units. They have many other interests, many other needs which should be fulfilled on the basis of participation and self-management outside the work units. In view of the progressive reduction of working hours, participation in production decisions may become less important, though it is the material basis for self-management in general. Thus, self-management is called for in other fields of life. The significance of self-management for democracy results from the fact that it allows the direct confrontation and reconciliation of different interests in achieving social goals or in satisfying individual and group needs. This is why we pay greater and greater attention to what we call the community of interests.

The Service Sector

Take, for example, the field of education or the health service, or any other public service. The field of health service deals with questions of the organization of a hospital, its work, and how it is geared to serve the needs of patients and of people. These are decided not by some department of a ministry of health but by bipartite committees on which you have, on the one hand, a representative of the patients or clients (their representative is a health insurance organization which is also represented by insurees themselves) and, on the other hand, representatives of the people who work in the hospital. This is an example of the principle of direct confrontation of interests and of democratic reconciliation and participation in finding solutions for different problems.

NEAL: How are the representatives of the patients elected?

PASIC: They are elected both at the local and the regional level. All people are insured, and we have annual meetings of the assembly of insurees which controls the work and administration of hospital organizations. And we have representatives of the health institutions such as hospitals. They sit together around a table and establish the conditions regarding cost of hospitalization, charges for the treatment of different diseases, and so on. In that way the patient, through his organization, has a right to control the conditions of work in hospitals and the quality of services.

NEAL: Do the patients, the "consumers" of health services, have the majority of votes? Can they really control?

PASIC: They are almost the same in number as the representatives of the institutions concerned. However, the patients, through their insurance organizations, are in a rather strong position because all the money for financing hospitals is in their hands. They are both the directors and the consumers. Thus you have a self-managed sovereignty of consumers realized through these organizations.

A similar scheme is applied to schools. We have, in that respect, copied some good old American traditions. In Europe, as you know, schools are governmental. They always have been under rather strict governmental control, such as the Ministry of Education, which is a very tyrannical institution. We try to de-statize the school system and give a greater scope to the general public, especially to those most directly concerned such as parents, and to enterprises who are interested in education, to influence the work of the school system and of particular scholastic institutions. So we have school boards which manage many matters of general concern to that particular institution. We also have something called the "community of interest" for education at the level of the commune, at the level of the local authority, and at the national level of the republic. I do not claim that all these assemblies function as one might desire ideally and that people are always willing to devote enough time to this work. On many occasions much depends on just a few very active and devoted people. In one case the school board functions very well indeed. In another it is just a pure form without any real content. We hope however that self-management is a process which will stimulate the development of consciousness and that bit by bit people will develop their self-management consciousness and readiness to devote their time to running their common business.

The Armed Forces

BRUCAN: How is the cost of the armed forces and of the whole state administrative apparatus covered on the basis of self-management principle in Yugoslavia?

PASIC: There was, up to the last constitutional amendments, a federal law which fixed the rules for taxation and the sources of taxation for different governmental bodies. Each commune had its own sources for taxation. They could tax land, for example, or they could have a turnover tax, and so on. These sources were fixed by law. Furthermore, different kinds of taxes were turned over to different bodies of government at different levels. The federal government was financed mainly from customs duties and from a turnover tax which was a very substantial source of income for the federal government. Since the federal government was and still is responsible for the army, the army was financed through the federal budget.

Now the situation is far more complicated since we have developed the system of people's defense, the People's Army. We have a standing army which is financed by the federal government, and we have territorial units which are financed by the local communities or by the different Republics. All these organs participate in financing these territorial forces. Each enterprise is obliged to have a kind of militia and to have some arms in case of war, in which case every unit should be able to defend itself. That is the realization of the Marxist idea of armed people instead of a professional army.

Of course, if you rely on that kind of a solution, you must trust your people.

External Pressures: The Soviet Union

BRUCAN: Can a society based on self-management emerge within a hostile external environment?

PASIC: The Yugoslav experience can speak for itself. The ability of a country to resist foreign intervention is greatly increased by developing self-management. If we had remained faithful to the Stalinist type of organization we could not have developed the force which was required to resist Stalinist pressure. You could not have raised that kind of support from the peasantry, the workers.

I think it is true that decisive steps in the direction of developing self-management were taken *after* the conflict with the Soviet Union had broken out. The question however is: what was the reason for that conflict itself? Why did Yugoslavia come into conflict with the USSR and its conception of how to build socialism? In our war of liberation the democratic forms we developed during the revolution were already the bases of future democratic structures and that is what caused Soviet reaction. The Soviet Union wanted to impose its model of central planning, and that was the source of the conflict itself. I agree that both in the Yugoslav case and in the case of China we have a departure from the Stalinist idea of democratic centralism as it had developed in the Soviet Union. We abandoned the Stalinist interpretation of democratic centralism. But one should bear in mind that democratic centralism could mean two completely different things, depending on where you apply that principle, whether it is applied to the whole sphere of political decision-making or only to the internal organization of the Communist Party. In Yugoslavia we tried to establish an independent self-management mechanism for the expression, democratic confrontation, and reconciliation of different interests which could function without day-to-day interference from outside by the League of Communists. That means that we tried to overcome the party monopoly in political decision-making and that is a complete departure from the Stalinist model of societal organization.

As for the internal organization of the party, we do not denounce the principle of democratic centralism but we try to emphasize the democratic elements in democratic centralism. One little illustration will show you what changes we have made. Previously, as in all Communist parties, in the Congresses of the Party, leadership imposed an obligatory guideline for the whole organization. Furthermore, we had similar congresses at the level of the republic and at the level of the communes, to apply Party decisions to the local conditions. Now we have changed that procedure completely. We start with meetings of the local authorities and work up from there to the national party congresses. On the basis of local decisions, we prepare the ground for a congress of the National League of Communists of Yugoslavia. So we try to go from bottom to top in decision-making, even in the Party.

The main concrete aim of the Chinese Cultural Revolution, by contrast, was to break the bureaucratic institutions of the political system; this was not in order to replace them with an independent democratic decision-making process, but to create more room for a charismatic leader who could really make decisions free from the institutional patterns of decision-making and the traditional bureaucratic structures of China. Thus, the ultimate goal of Mao Tse-Tung is the building of a communist society as he imagines it. But the means that he chose are those of a limited charismatic leader.

Let us turn to Eastern Europe. I think Rumania, Hungary, Bulgaria, and Eastern Germany are all rather far away from the Yugoslav experience. The fear they have of self-management is that it establishes a managerial stratum of people who feel independent of the political mechanism. Thus the danger of self-management for governments like those of Eastern Europe is not so much external as it is internal: self-management is perceived as a threat by the people in power.

THORSRUD: I tend to be skeptical about the causal relationship Professor Pasic indicated: that, because of decentralized self-management, you were able to build the forces necessary to resist the pressure from the Soviet Union. Could an alternative causal relationship exist? Because of the pressure from the Soviet Union, Yugoslavia was able to build up the self-management system. What I suggest is really that causes and effects are far from simple. In fact, from the local experiments I have seen, I would conclude that it is very hard to start a learning process in a radical way without a certain degree of pressure on the individual level, on the group level, on the organizational level, and maybe on the state level. Self-management, seen as a learning process, depends on an optimum level of outside pressure. There are similar indications for the Israeli kibbutz movement.

The Market Pressures

ASHMORE: I take it that the self-management system as it developed in Yugoslavia depends on the market: that there is a certain amount of decision-making that results from a market process?

NEAL: This is correct. At the production level you have to have the market in order to have decentralization.

ASHMORE: I suppose the market also provides a kind of objective test of the self-management program.

NEAL: Yes. If an enterprise is not able to operate efficiently, profitably, ultimately it goes down the drain. As a matter of fact, that is what has happened to a considerable extent in Yugoslavia.

PARDO: I wonder whether self-management can continue to exist in view of the pressures from the West in the sense of market forces, the pressure to export. This is a constant pressure which may force a transformation of the system.

ADIZES: I think the Yugoslav system, provided that the capital and labor-mobility problem is solved, will be able to compete better than the hierarchical organizational structures of the West because of the ability to modernize and change structures, which is much greater than in the West. In the West, it takes consultants and millions of dollars to change a simple organization. In Yugoslavia, it takes just so many meetings, and the system is geared for change.

PACEK: To reply to Dr. Pardo's question: I must admit that there is a very real pressure from the West. We do maintain the market system. We know that not to maintain a market system would be an oddity; it would mean not to participate in the world economy. On the other hand, there is a question of solving the problem of distribution of income which arises from this type of economic cooperation.

We have to build an economic system in such a way that the principle that everyone is rewarded by his real work should remain valid. Every one of us knows that the market does not divide the income according to the input of work. That is well known and I do not need to remind you of monopolies, etc. If we want to be able, in a condition of equality, to trade with all other nations we must have and protect an internal system which respects the principles of reward of real work of the people as a whole.

BORGESE: Two questions have been raised. First, whether a system as complex as self-management can resist the pressures of what I think are three kinds of environmental stresses; and, second, if it resists, whether it can be effective in terms of production.

With regard to the first question, the first type of environmental stress is military power from outside. I think it has been convincingly shown in the discussion here that a decentralized self-management system may well be the very best system to resist such pressures or to maintain itself in the fight against vastly superior military forces. This has been the experience of the partisans, the experience of the Vietcong, and in general, it can be demonstrated that a decentralized system is more stable. I think it is quite conceivable that the Vietcong lesson carries over at least to some extent to the resistance against other environmental stresses.

The second type of stress that has been mentioned is infiltration of capitalist market forces. This is a relatively new development and, as Professor Adizes has pointed out, we just cannot tell how it is going to work out.

The third type of stress we have not even touched upon. That is the stress coming from problems which transcend the decision-making range of the self-managing unit. Problems such as pollution or the impact of technology. I suspect that these pressures may force the self-managing system to be more aggressive and more expansive, in order not to be crushed by them.

On the second question, that of productivity, we may even grant that there is a certain amount of waste built into such a very complex system. Perhaps it may even slow down the rate of growth in some, although the record of the Yugoslav economy does not give any such indication. Even if it were so, it would not really matter, however. We should then compare the waste built into the self-managing system with the waste built into the system of free enterprise or the waste built into a centralized economy. Also, we hear a lot these days about the enhancement of quality instead of quantity, and although this argument often makes me suspicious since it is usually advanced by people who have reached a quite satisfactory quantitative level of consumption, there can be no doubt that the self-management system produces values which cannot be measured in terms of money alone.

INITIATING SELF-MANAGEMENT
Necessity for Committed Leadership

ADIZES: Self-management, as with any planned change of some magnitude, is a difficult process to maintain, nourish, and make successful. I would say that if there is an external threat which moves on such a weak body before it successfully develops immunities, it will destroy it.

The Peruvian experience leads me to believe that in order to be able to establish self-management, to make the process successful, a committed, prolonged, open-minded, and secure leadership is needed at the top.

WHEELER: As far as I can tell from the discussion, self-management is something that does not arise on a basis of or because of demands from the people who are ultimately going to be the self-managers. On the contrary, it appears that self-management is imposed from the authoritarian, previously hierarchical position.

This is not really surprising to me because in the history of democracy, democracy itself does not arise on the basis of a demand from the people to have a voice in government. It moves from the top down.

Necessity for Grass Roots Support

PASIC: I strongly disagree with the statement that the self-management system in Yugoslavia was imposed from above. It would not have been possible to build our self-management system if it could not rely on the already created wide political mobilization and self-initiative of the masses. This was achieved during the war of liberation and during the revolution. Without that spirit no one could impose and successfully develop the self-management pattern of organization.

In Czechoslovakia too there was a strong movement toward the establishment of Workers Councils. There are people like Ota Sik, with whom I had the opportunity of speaking, who feel that one of the big mistakes of Czech leadership and Dubcek was that they did not rely enough on this initiative of the workers, on this movement toward establishing industrial democracy and workers' control in factories. Instead the Czechs relied more on the political-intellectual wing of the movement which proved to be less resistant and less reliable in a moment of crisis than a mass movement of the workers would have been.

All these cases, I think, show that self-management is not just invented by leadership but that it lies deep in the concepts of the people; and the creation of workers' councils in these socialist countries is in some cases a continuous reaction against the administrative centralized system which deprives them of all initiative.

Restructuring Work

McWHINNEY: I should like to analyze the question of how to start a self-management system from a different angle.

There are strong political reasons for beginning with the work place. The work place is the most important factor in all economies; it is a leverage point if you look for social change. But we should also consider the need for developing self-management in the community outside of the work place. In American society today, the most promising area is the community of art and personal creativity.

Our technologies have changed, in this country as well as in many others, even if they are not yet as highly automated. Our technology is fundamentally different from what it was 100 years ago, and probably quite significantly different from what it was even thirty years ago.

There is no longer any technological justification for a two-class system, that is, workers and management. There is instead a social and perhaps political justification for change. If we do not get this fact straight, we shall keep trying to use social forces to maintain technological obsolescence in terms of work structuring as well as educational structuring.

Starting with the individual worker with a task design, and working directly through the system at the bottom as opposed to setting up countervailing political forces such as unions or political governmental structures, we find we can get at a real reduction in bureaucracy.

Our experience is that this works. We can achieve industrial democracy by taking out of the hierarchy those people whose job it was traditionally to supervise. We found that when we removed supervision, we obtained, in the first place, a tremendous reduction in cost of output. Thus, to start with, we have a really substantial economic justification. In some cases this amounted to fifty percent of the overhead cost of operating, if you calculate the cost not only of the supervising person which you can eliminate, but the whole concept of supervision, getting rid of the supervisory role of the manager who is paid $30,000 a year all the way up through the organization. But you have to start at the bottom. If you don't start at the bottom the system is corrupt. We have to start from the bottom and eliminate supervision, redesign the job of the manager, eliminate intrusion downwards, the habit of telling workers what to do, of not trusting them, of not letting people be themselves, as workers, as students, as teachers, whatever role it may be. Then we shall have a much more efficient operation in economic terms; and, at the same time, we shall have a system that offers potential for participation not limited to the work environment but extending to the community as a whole.

McCOY: I would like to list a few prerequisites for the establishment of self-management in learning, especially within the university which, I think, holds the greatest potential for moving society toward self-management through education.

(1) In the personal dimension we need individuals who see persons and their fulfillment as the supreme value and who are willing to struggle for maximum freedom and responsibility for each human being.

(2) Organizationally we need a faculty and administrators who view the students as colearners, and who understand that sharing decision-making with them is part of a community enterprise. This means that learning will be viewed as a process of developing competency for problem solving, not as a mere assimilation of information. It will mean that the building of a curriculum, the admissions process, the evaluation of teaching and learning, the appointment of faculty and the formulation of budgets, the formation of committees, are all potential learning processes in which the students can share.

(3) Community can be established in the University by decentralizing into relatively autonomous college units of 200 to 400 persons. The ratio of faculty to students should not be over 15 to one. Community develops when students and faculty share common concerns and make decisions on a cooperative basis. Authority is derived from competence and knowledge, not by external means. Community in learning requires trust and openness, a laboratory climate, effective advisory and counseling relationships, and a pervasive concern for mutuality in growth.

(4) One condition for the establishment of self-management is financial independence so that external forces cannot interfere with internal objectives and processes. This can be realized if students pay their full cost of education or through philanthropic financial support with no strings attached.

(5) Self-management is not an end in itself. In educational terms it is a means to enhance the development of each person. Maximum growth is realized through maximum responsibility.

(6) There are some dangers inherent in self-management in education: some students interpret it to mean freedom of choice and action regardless of social consequences. Faculty as well as students must be educated to use self-correction in lieu of correction by traditional methods. If a college or university operates on the basis of self-management, graduates may have difficulty operating in other institutions based on different principles. Self-management will not work without self-discipline, including a sense of responsibility toward others as well as oneself.

Whatever the potential pitfalls, the advantages derived make the risks worthwhile.

The General Conditions

PARDO: I think there are a certain number of essential conditions if any experiment in self-management is to succeed. One of these is that every individual in the society must be convinced that he, as an individual, has a responsibility to society. This is quite different from the American concept of overemphasis on rights and very little emphasis on any responsibility of individuals to society. Self-management cannot exist in this climate. There must be a general recognition of individual responsibility to the community and to society. In turn, of course, the community has certain responsibilities to the individual. Generally speaking I would think that self-management has a vital role to play in the world, particularly since it tends to relieve the overpressures of the societal structure on the individual. Whether this concept should be the same in all branches of the economy is something that has not yet been proven. It also will have to be shown yet whether self-management will have a significant impact in the global context.

PASIC: I should like to discuss a few questions that have come up frequently in our talks these last days. I also should like to try to qualify my own statements on these issues.

Let me first take up the questions. Is self-management a product of special historical coincidence of circumstances or is it something that is a universal trend of our time? Is experience created in different countries relevant to other countries or not?

These two questions are interrelated. So is the question as to whether it is possible to impose a model of self-management on a society and under what conditions; or is self-management a response to spontaneous demands and pressures from below?

All these questions can be answered if we think of self-management not as a definite normative and institutional structure or ready-made model, but in much broader terms, as a complex historical response to some deep and vital changes in our times.

We live in a world in which the social environment becomes more and more complex. With the development of modern technology, individuals find the conditions of their lives determined by huge organizations— economic, political, and other. These hierarchical structures are very difficult to control in a democratic way. The traditional means of representative democracy are no longer effective. On the other hand, we live in a world of widespread literacy and education. The masses of people are no longer what they used to be one hundred years ago, and personal aspirations of people have grown tremendously. In this contradictory situation, new ways must be found for the individual to fulfill himself and to acquire more direct control over the conditions of his own life. Self-management offers a variety of answers to this challenge, depending on different conditions in different parts of the world. Although this world is divided into different political systems and different levels of economic development there are nevertheless some common characteristics, and self-management therefore is universally relevant. It represents a kind of response to these vital challenges of our time.

Thus I believe that we have something to learn from each other and that the questions arising from self-management are relevant to all of us, regardless of the political system in which we are living and no matter whether we live in a developed or semideveloped or undeveloped country. Self-management in this respect is like democracy in general. You could never agree on its definition if you tried to identify democracy with a definite set of institutional structures. You have to have a much broader approach. Self-management has a revolutionary driving force within itself. You cannot hope to develop self-management on any scale and, at the same time, preserve the existing political and economic structure. If you take a conservative stand, you have to oppose self-management because a self-management system is an attack on the hierarchical structure of every unit of society, of every institution. It erodes the hierarchical structure, it erodes centralism, it puts people into a position where they can control the conditions of their life. People who are in such a position are completely different social beings from the abstract citizen of whom Marx spoke. A man who can control his immediate environment will not stop there. He will demand direct influence on the broader issues.

In the light of the experience in my own country, I know that it is impossible to confine self-management to the grass roots level. You have to take into account its broader social and political effects.

BRUCAN: Let me state from the very outset that in my view self-management belongs to the future rather than to the present, and that talking about self-management today is, as we say in Rumania, like selling the fur of the bear while he is still in the woods. However, in its embryonic state in Yugoslavia, self-management is a major revolutionary experiment that is going to have an ever-growing impact on contemporary society, both in the East and in the West.

Having said this, I wish to make four points. (1) Self-management is basically an internal phenomenon. Its emergence, evolution, and success depend, however, to a large extent on the external environment and its pressures. (2) Self-management at the level of global society requires decentralization of power, a gradual withering away of the state and its machinery. This is a condition that is inconceivable within the present world power structure. (3) Self-management of the economy will be historically ripe after the executive type of management in corporations has exhausted its potentialities and the economy acquires the highest technological development. (4) Internal and external historical conditions in Yugoslavia have resulted in a dualistic structure in which self-management at the factory and community level coexists with a particular form of centralized power at the top.

Let me briefly substantiate this point.

Self-management in Yugoslavia has its roots in the national liberation war and in the revolution against capitalist exploitation and oppression. Nevertheless, immediately after the war Yugoslavia, like the other Eastern European countries, adopted the Soviet model of economic and political organization. Under the then-prevailing circumstances this seemed the safest thing to do. It was only the tension in Soviet-Yugoslav relations of 1948 that encouraged the self-management movement and stimulated it as an answer to the Soviet model which could help the national and revolutionary forces in Yugoslavia to remake society in their own way and thus to withstand better the external pressures. Essentially, in my opinion, it was the same underlying motivation that launched the Cultural Revolution in China. The Chinese wanted to destroy the political structure initially built in accordance with the Soviet model, but which no longer fit the new orientation of China in world politics, particularly in its relations with the Soviet Union. This external element is essential in understanding the problem.

Yugoslavia, however, could not and did not avoid the problems an underdeveloped country has to face when building socialism. Briefly, in such countries domestic backward conditions of the economy, illiteracy, lack of traditional democratic processes in public life, and external competition from the advanced Western nations compelled revolutionary governments to place their nation on something like a war footing against existing conditions. Their plan was to attack the deficiency of backwardness and defend the newly conquered position against external pressures with all the will and ardor of a military contest. The political solution adopted thus far in dealing with such formidable tasks has not been the withering away of the state as anticipated by Marx, but rather the strengthening of the state, including highly centralized and all-out planning of the economy. The by-products of such a political structure have been stringent limitations on political opposition and intellectual stiflement, all initially directed against the class enemy but eventually used also to enforce social conformity throughout the whole nation.

As you may know, Marx's anticipation was built on the assumption that the socialist revolution would take place on a world scale, starting with the most developed nations. Under such conditions self-management or self-administration was envisaged as a social system in a society that had attained a gigantic development of productive forces, a high degree of democracy, and universal literacy. Therefore Marshal Tito, in his own way, was confronted with Lenin's dilemma before the Russian Revolution: should he wait until the historical conditions were ripe or start right away with all the risks and compromises involved? The courageous decision to introduce self-management was made and that decision will go down in history as a landmark.

But we must assess the experiment realistically, with all the consequences inherent in any jump in historical developments. Let me illustrate the case with just one example: the role of trade unions mentioned here in the discussion. If self-management is a fact in society then there is no need for unions anymore. For what role can unions play when there are no classes and no employers or managers, when all members of society have learned how to govern themselves and have taken this business into their own hands as is supposed to happen in a society based on self-management? Against whom should trade unions defend the interests of the workingman in a self-management system?

With regard to the economic infrastructure of self-management, it certainly requires two basic preconditions. One is social ownership, by which I mean abolition of private ownership of means of production and eventually of any and every kind of property. Second, it requires the highest technology available at any given time. I will quote what Kardelj had to say recently at the Serajevo Congress in 1971: "Only after having assured the reliance on automatic production services will society be able to organize itself completely as a self-managing society which will no longer require either state coercion or coercion in the production process which today requires manual work." As for self-management in countries with a capitalist structure, and with a welfare state or industrial democracy as Norway, I can only say that the concept should not be applied exclusively in social and economic terms. What counts in the last analysis is the political variable: who holds the power in society? Self-management is real only when the answer is, "Nobody."

SOME EMERGING PROBLEMS

PASIC: In implementing the self-management ideas, however, Yugoslavia has had some serious economic, political, and social difficulties.

I shall just mention briefly a few of the problems we are facing at this stage of development. First of all, we noted a process of social differentiation and the emergence of new social inequalities. Market mechanisms which are indispensable at this stage of development (and we have no illusions that we either could or should abolish that mechanism) tend to distort the principles of distribution according to work done. Due to that fact there are in Yugoslavia rich and poor enterprises, privileged and underprivileged branches of economy, which brings about a sharpening of contradictions between the more and the less developed parts of the country.

A second series of problems is connected with the tendencies of partialization and territorial autarchy. Conditions of life and satisfaction of needs of individuals and groups sometimes depend too much on the position of the territorial community to which they belong. What quality of health service an individual will enjoy depends on the wealth of the community in which he lives.

A third series of difficulties stems from the contrast between the extremely large potentiality for expressing different interests at all levels of social organization, and the rather narrow channels through which these interests can be transformed into effective political demands in political decision-making.

There is still a duality in our system. Self-management is fairly well developed at the grass roots level, at the level of the individual self-managed unit; but as for the global organization of society, the state still plays a very important role. This is obvious from the very detailed legislation governing different enterprises, branches of the economy, and so on. By changing these laws you can change overnight the position of an enterprise, creating uncertainty among workers and weakening their real social position.

This legislation is rather extensive. From 1965 until 1970 we had in our federal assemblies 250 laws per year, almost a law a day.

Another set of problems arises from the lack of self-management mechanisms for solving inevitable contradictions in the working of the economy and in the process of economic reproduction.

Thus we have passed a series of constitutional amendments to find solutions for these problems. With these amendments we have made a decisive attempt to make self-management into a homogeneous global system of socialist organization.

The absolutely crucial problem for self-management in Yugoslavia is to find a solution to the problem of the concentration and circulation of what one could call social capital or means of reproduction. We try to solve this problem by strengthening the basic unit of our associated work, the basic self-management cells of our society.

Workers in the elementary units of associated work now have the ability to control not only the part of the income they create for their personal income and for current production, but also the part which is used in investment in other enterprises, in banks, credit systems, and so on. And in that way we hope to encourage also the voluntary integration of different units of associated work. Workers in a smaller enterprise no longer have any reason to be afraid that by joining a big enterprise they will be deprived of their autonomy, of their right to control their own income. Thus, this basic unit of associated work should be an efficient instrument to control the management of big enterprises from the inside and to fight in that way against technocratic tendencies.

A second line which we follow in trying to solve the problems I spoke of is to develop a mechanism of so-called self-management accords and social agreements. These are collective agreements in which the self-managed enterprises, the bodies of public authority, the trade unions, or other interested parties come together and regulate questions of common interest. They fix the criteria for internal distribution of income in order to eliminate the big differences in income for the same work. They regulate questions of how the enterprises should jointly solve the problem of redundant labor and similar questions. There is a list of problems which have to be dealt with in that way and this has been fixed by the Constitution itself. We cannot hope to eliminate overnight all these problems and difficulties. What we can hope for is to proceed in such a manner as to strengthen constantly the position of the worker in associated labor while not strengthening the governmental authorities which would regulate these problems from outside.

The Role of Professional Management in Self-Management

ADIZES: One of the constitutional amendments, No. 15, allows enterprises to determine internally the decision-making processes within certain constraints determined by the Constitution. The result is that quite a few companies have enlarged the mandate of representatives on the workers council. They have also eliminated one of the self-managerial bodies, the Governing Board, and replaced it with the Collegium which is a body of professional executives. These two developments have resulted in the strengthening of the executive within each organization. This is possible since there is no real operative definition of self-management. We all know what it should be. But when the time comes to design strategies which will achieve desired goals, without operative terms to work with, there are constant adaptations which may turn out not to be universally acceptable. For instance, what is management, not to speak of self-management? In Yugoslavia terminology—and that is where the difficulty of the 15th Amendment and its implications comes in—the meaning of "management" covers both policy-making decisions and administrative decisions. Policy-making decisions which are crucial to the life of the community in general are made by the general community, and the administrative decisions of implementation are made by the professional managers. I think that this approach is really derived from the central planning model from which self-management departed. In the central planning model all decisions are made at the center and thereafter the managers only administer. Self-management just turned this principle upside down: all decisions are made at the bottom by workers, and the managers still only administer. But the distinction between what is administration and what is policy is very difficult to make. The two areas are overlapping. In a cumulative form, administrative decisions might have policy repercussions. Even in the United States we hear the cry that the executive function is usurping powers from the legislative; the same phenomenon is occurring in Yugoslavia.

This artificial distinction between policy and administration works as long as there is central planning or some form of control over the environment. When decisions must be adapted to a changing environment, those who possess the information, and the knowledge to manipulate it, have the power as well. In a changing environment, time spent in decision-making becomes a crucial factor. Suppose that managers, in their capacity as administrators, have to go through the same ponderous democratic process of achieving consensus that is required for policy decision-making. By the time a consensus has been achieved, the environment has changed and the consensus must be changed as well. It all turns out to be a very difficult process for the managers. Thus it became clear that a better distinction between policy and administrative decisions is necessary, a result of which is the 15th Amendment. The opposition to the managerial changes which resulted from the 15th Amendment stemmed, in my opinion, from an oversimplified view of the role of management in organizations, an oversimplified view of the pressures on managers to make decisions in a competitive environment.

BORGESE: How do you see the role of the manager in a self-managing enterprise?

ADIZES: He has to be an entrepreneur and he has to be a leader. These are two different characteristics. Leadership is the capability to communicate a message and mobilize the group to follow to a goal. Entrepreneurship is the ability to identify opportunities involving risk and design strategies to exploit them.

A leader who is not an entrepreneur mobilizes the group, gives them an esprit de corps and a goal, but he does this for some riskless kind of opportunity. This is not going to work because in the long run, in a competitive environment, unless you undertake risk you stagnate. Once the results are disappointing, the followers cease to identify with the leader and he loses his position, but meanwhile, he might have destroyed the company's future.

An entrepreneur who is not a leader, on the other hand, identifies opportunities but may not be able to mobilize the masses, to make the group identify with his individual risk-taking, and so a credibility gap develops. No matter how good the economic returns, the workers feel that it is the entrepreneur who has the power and who makes decision for them, and they do not necessarily identify with the results. If the results turn unsatisfactory at any point in time, even if due to uncontrollable conditions or windfall effects, this enterprise is going to experience major labor-relation difficulties since the workers do not identify themselves with the decisions made in the company and do not feel committed to them. Thus, in the self-management system, a professional manager, working within a competitive environment, has to be both an entrepreneur and a leader.

It appears to me from my study that leadership needs can be satisfied in a communal system because of the intrinsic rewards of experiencing leadership. But the satisfaction of economic entrepreneurial needs is extremely difficult to provide in a group decision-making and a group-reward distribution system.

Enforcement of Self-Management Rights

WHEELER: Are there any cases in the courts in which workers bring suit against an enterprise claiming that it is not running according to the constitution? And if so, does this help define self-management in operative terms?

PASIC: The individual rights of the workers are protected by the courts, and this is a rather widespread practice. We have very numerous cases in Yugoslavia, thousands and thousands of them, in which workers who are fired by management go to a court and claim that there was no justification for their being fired. The court very often rescinds the decision of the workers' council which decided the firing, and the workers have to be taken back and paid for the time they were out.

WHEELER: What about a worker who claims that the enterprise is not being run democratically? Can he bring suit charging the enterprise with being an undemocratic enterprise?

PASIC: He can do that through a constitutional court, or he can do it politically, or through a tribunal, which is very often done. If he wants to go to the law, he must go to the constitutional court of either the republic or the federation. There, workers may claim that their constitutional rights of self-management have not been applied, observed, and respected. The constitutional courts are really overburdened with such cases. There are more than we had foreseen. We thought that the constitutional court would deal more with questions as to whether the laws and regulations made by local authority are in accordance with state laws, and less with this type of violation. But in practice people approach quite a lot of these constitutional courts at the republic and at the federation level.

ECHEVERRIA: Two questions. 1) Does the self-managing worker not cease to identify with the working class as such? 2) Does all the information in an enterprise reach every single sector sufficiently and is there sufficient time to self-manage?

PASIC: The aim of the whole process of liberation of labor is indeed that the working class should not be a separate class in the society but that all people should become self-managers. In that way, to use Marx's term, the working class abolishes itself and abolishes the conditions of class society in general. The aim is that we should not have a separate working class, principally of manual workers, but that all people should be workingmen, with the same way of earning income, the same rights to manage according to their work. What we are afraid of at this moment are the deviations and inequalities within the working class which do emerge, and which I have mentioned before, from certain monopolies and privileges linked to the market economy. These are problems that have to be dealt with in order to preserve the basic solidarity of the working people and to overcome the negative repercussions of economic competition between and among different economic units.

PACEK: Almost every statute regulating the internal relations of an enterprise contains something about the system of information in the enterprise. But this is a complex problem. Everyone in the enterprise knows the schedule and agenda of the Working Council and the conclusions and decisions are distributed to everyone. The question, however, is what kind of information places the workers in the position of finding the right solution for a problem? This is an educational process and it is not unusual that after the members of the workers' council have been elected, they have seminars for days and days to get used to making decisions.

Another problem arises from the fact that information is filtered through the managing board or the managing staff, and as it is filtered, it often happens that it is put in a way that favors the interests and standpoints of the managing staff. So the problem is that the self-managers must get direct information on the most important questions in connection with the society in a commune as a whole.

Is Social Ownership Necessary?

ADIZES: When we talk about workers' commitment to self-management, it is assumed that this kind of commitment is achieved through social ownership. It is perceived that the Peruvian worker who feels that he owns will work harder and manage. In Yugoslavia, since the worker owns the results of his work, he is supposedly more committed. In a kibbutz you have the same hidden assumption.

I think that the assumption that a commitment to work is related to the ownership prerogative is erroneous. There are still strikes in Yugoslavia. If all problems—the firing of management, the norms of production, the salaries—can be settled by workers, why do they still strike?

I found impressive similarities between Yugoslav strikes and the student sit-ins in American colleges. First, it is only a minority that is striking. Second, no bargaining is taking place. It is a sit-in, or as Bogdan Kavcic called it, it is a show of dissatisfaction, since although the minority feels they should have a say on major decisions via the democratic process, they cannot effectively implement these decisions via the democratic channels as they exist.

Thus, I think that a commitment to an organization is the result of the ability to effectuate decisions and not a result of legalistic ownership rights. The management group, even if not in an ownership position in the United States, very often feels very committed to the organization because it is a creation of its labors. The workers in Yugoslavia, on the other hand, own the results of their work but do not feel that they can affect those results, that they can actually manage. Social ownership does not give them everything. The fact is that there are strikes in Yugoslav companies. Workers in a sense strike against their own company. Thus social ownership does not necessarily increase commitment, but it might have negative repercussions in that it might affect labor and capital mobility if exercised the way the Yugoslavs practice it.

In Yugoslavia, the society at large owns the resources, and the members of each industrial community own the results of their work. No company may decrease the value of its assets; because if it could, workers could decide to sell the company, distribute the revenues, and go to the next company, sell it, distribute it, etc. Labor can only own the results of its work; it cannot decrease the value of the accumulated assets.

Now, let us assume that you are a member of this community and for the last ten years you have voted each time to distribute a high portion of the net income for investments instead of personal income. Ten years later, you decide you want to move somewhere else. You have no ownership rights over the accumulation of your past sacrifices; and this might create a problem for labor mobility.

True, there is a new constitutional amendment which will change this situation. However, the mechanism has not been established yet. In my opinion the amendment will eventually lead to the negation of social ownership. In a capitalist society when you sell a stock on the market the value of the stock is what buyers perceive to be the future fruits of the seller's past investments. So the seller realizes the future fruits in the selling price of his stock. Maybe the Eastern Europeans are going to develop the People's Stock Market, rather than the Wall Street Stock Market. But there is eventually going to be a stock market in Yugoslavia, to facilitate labor and capital mobility, and that will negate social ownership *as they have it now.*

Without developed capital markets, without adequate labor mobility, the economic results will not be as effective as they would otherwise be. Rigid capital and labor markets mean concentration of economic power, and that will not help self-management.

PACEK: Professor Adizes made a distinction between social ownership on the one hand and self-management on the other. According to the Yugoslav constitution, social ownership is not a practical antithesis of private property. Social ownership of the productive means in our country already includes self-management.

Mr. Adizes raised the issue of the ownership of the fruits of past labor. This is considered to be a very serious problem in Yugoslavia. The recent constitutional amendments offer a new approach: it is not only income from present work that must be shared. The worker must also get his share of the accumulated investments.

WHEELER: Will that be some kind of a supplementary income payment? Something like a rent that society would pay individuals for the use of their capital?

PACEK: The credit relationship is different. The investors have no right to interfere in self-management and in those collectives which should manage independently the means of production. That is the difference between a private shareholder and shareholders in our system who get only a limited profit for the money that they have invested. There has been some discussion on setting up councils of creditors, but they would be advisory only, without decision-making power.

ADIZES: It is an interesting point. The Yugoslavs have reversed the situation under capitalism. A capitalist society claims to give workers a fixed income and riskless conditions. Capital undertakes risk and then benefits from a varying return on investment. In Yugoslavia, labor undertakes risk and benefits from varied income while capital is riskless and is allocated a fixed return. In the United States labor now claims that its role is not riskless and thus it wants participation and a say in company matters. The same is true for capital in Yugoslavia.

Eventually the need to justify paying somebody back for his past sacrifices which can be transferable will lead to a mechanism for enjoying the prerogatives of private property. No one gives money without strings attached whenever risk is involved. Capital in Yugoslavia bears risk too, and once the inevitable strings are attached, it means that capital will share not only in the distribution of rewards, something already recognized, but also in the prerogatives of management and decision-making, a fact yet to be recognized.

PASIC: Social ownership means that there are laws which exclude any distribution of managerial prerogatives (and power) of appropriation of income which is based on anything but work done. Work with socially owned means of production can be organized *only* according to the principles of self-management.

ADIZES: To say that capital should not have any prerogatives of management is conceptually as limited as to say—as we do say in the United States—that labor should not have managerial prerogatives. What we should be looking for in self-management is that *all* interest groups that contribute should share in the managerial prerogatives.

BORGESE: Social ownership does not mean that the workers must own the means of production in the classical sense, including *ius utendi* and *abutendi.* That does not really matter. The concept of social ownership is that *no one else must be allowed to own them.* If there were an owner other than the worker, the owner might sell the company over the workers' heads or he might fire the workers or otherwise govern their use of various resources. I think the basic concept of self-management excludes the possibility of anyone in general owning the resources or the means of production. This I think is the merit of the Yugoslav theory that it has spelled out the connection, has made it organic, between the concept of nonappropriability and the concept of self-management. I think that we are going to live more and more with this concept of the non-appropriability of resources in the context of resource management, energy management, management of technology, of information and communications, etc. It is from this angle that I think that studies on the organic connection between nonappropriability and self-management become mandatory.

Returning now to the preceding discussion: it seems to me that once you have postulated the merger between social capital and labor, i.e., that social capital cannot be *owned* by anybody and can be *managed* only by labor, the worker who produces it, then the question of the rights of capital to participate in decision-making as its managerial prerogative simply cannot arise. In this sense, the Yugoslav situation is *not* a "reversal" of the Western situation. It is different altogether.

ADIZES: What was the ownership system in the companies in Norway where industrial democracy was introduced?

THORSRUD: The companies are all privately owned except one, which is owned jointly by the government and private interests, 50 percent each. We have been invited to work in government-owned companies now, but we have not found any significant difference between private and governmentally owned enterprises in terms of their systems participation.

ADIZES: Was there—if you can isolate that factor just for analysis—any difference in the difficulties, in the reaction of management, between the various companies depending on the ownership system?

THORSRUD: The patterns of investment and markets with which the state-owned companies are dealing are so simple that I would not like to do these experiments in these companies. I would rather do them in companies with a much more rapid change of capital and market, because we want severe tests. We now have comparative work on the level of workers' representation on the Boards, and there is no sign whatsoever that there is any difference between the privately owned and the state-owned companies when it comes to the mechanisms of formal participation. The roles of people on the boards are exactly the same.

ADIZES: I am trying to focus on the issue of whether the pattern of ownership is really significant for the development of the type of participatory system that you are talking about. If I understand you correctly, there is no significant difference.

THORSRUD: Your question calls for a further clarification. You really cannot discuss this without discussing the changing nature of capital itself.

In Norway the situation was different in two basic ways from what it was in Yugoslavia when the system of participation was initiated there. First, in Norway there was a new generation of professional managers, with quite different values and powers because of the information at their disposal. That was lacking in Yugoslavia in 1945. It existed in Norway since 1950. Second, capital has been redefined in a very fundamental way by the fact that any professional manager has a number of choices for raising capital, from banks, government, from outside and inside. Finally, capital is not only concrete capital in terms of money and machines and buildings. Capital in Norway is also abstract capital, namely, trust in a network of people who in different institutions (including Unions) have privileged access to capital. So I have answered your question in a very complicated way, the only way I can answer it.

I do indeed accept that traditional private ownership has to be redefined, that it is in fact being redefined in many countries. Social control of resources must be redefined to include control over capital, both in a concrete and in an abstract sense. I am not talking now only about natural resources, productive resources, human resources, but about an even more important resource—access to a network of information and trust. Unless we redefine capital and resources in this way, I think we are thinking too much about the last thirty years and not at all about the next thirty years. There is, in fact, a change taking place in social control in many countries, particularly some with mixed economies who have gone through a stage of welfare economy for some time. The new generation of managers are defining leadership in institutional terms, and not in narrowly economic terms.

The Role of Trade Unions

THORSRUD: Mr. Pasic, do you think the unions in Yugoslavia have become stronger or weaker during these last ten years?

Compared to Scandinavian Trade Unions, they seem to have lost most of the traditional trade union bases. Have they lost their influence on the income of their members? My suggestion is based on my impressions ten years ago.

Have they recovered any of that? Or are these problems still handled through other channels—the Workers' Councils and the cost accounting on the company level?

Secondly, do the trade unions hold a distinctively different type of function in your political system from the party?

I am very skeptical about any monolithic system. Formerly you had some possibility of using the trade unions as a complementary system vis-a-vis the party on some levels. Do you still have that? And how do the unions operate?

PASIC: To the surprise of many people, not only outside Yugoslavia but inside, the role of the trade unions has been greatly increased. Many people in Yugoslavia believed that in a system of self-management we should no longer need trade unions, or that they would be limited to petty matters. But that was not so. Ten years ago, as a matter of fact, the role of the trade unions was very restricted. But that was a transitional period. We were emerging from an administrative system in which the Party was the central decision-making body, the leading elite organization; all other organizations were just the tools of the Party to implement its policy.

We have overcome that system with decentralization. Then the question arose of whether we needed trade unions at all. But practice has demonstrated that we cannot do without trade unions, without facing serious problems like strikes, and unorganized forms of dissatisfaction which existed in different communities. Workers' Councils, even when they are elected by and composed of workers, may acquire managerial biases. They are easily impressed by what management tells them about investment needs, and they are sometimes inclined to neglect the rights and needs of some groups of people outside the enterprise. So the trade unions are needed as a tool to resist such violations of people's rights. And thus something of the classical role of the trade unions is reemerging now. There are proposals that we should put into the constitution, that trade unions should have a right to sue the management of an enterprise or the

Workers' Councils for violating the rights of individuals or group members of such unions.

THORSRUD: What particular values do the trade unions stand for? For instance, do they stand for the protection of specialized trades or guilds? What is their attitude to wildcat strikes? Do they cultivate autonomy in work groups?

PASIC: It depends on the concrete situation. There have been situations in which trade unions were on the side of the strikers, and there have been some where they opposed them. During the big strikes in the mining industries in Bosnia, for example, the unions sided with the workers.

The trade unions have acquired a very important role in self-management which I have briefly mentioned in my paper: the mechanism of making so-called self-management accords and social agreements. Trade unions are an equal partner in these, and they should take a broader view comprising the interests of the whole branch of workers, a broader community of working in bargaining. It is their function to keep the balance between the well-off enterprises and the poor enterprises, to insist on establishing some obligatory standards for distribution of income, etc. Thus they play a considerable role in reducing the income gaps which have emerged in our country. It happens that men of the same skill, and for the same amount of work, are paid twice as much if they work in a company which makes profits than if they work in a company which is less fortunate.

And they have yet another role to play. They function as the organizing instrument of the workers at the level of central decision-making, in the parliaments of the republics and in the federal assemblies. They express themselves on almost every measure taken by the government. They pronounce themselves on questions of housing, rents, on the increase of prices of food, and so on. They very often put strong pressure on the government and make sure that these problems should be solved in favor of the interests of the poorest among the workers.

These are the three functions of the unions today. In general, their importance has been increasing in the last few years. They will remain an important part of the whole self-management system.

THORSRUD: The real question is: what sort of new goals do we generate? What is the function of the unions in this respect? Do they claim and advance other values than those traditionally emerging from a business environment? For instance, do they ask value questions like: what happens to the Yugoslav workers if they have to work on the same type of technology as the American auto workers? Do they get involved in the effects of the immediate work situation?

PACEK: My personal opinion is that our trade unions have too many opinions, not too few. The papers are full of debates on all the questions you mentioned: overwork, anything from housing to prices, inequalities in income, and so on. The trade unions should represent the common interests of the working people as a whole.

This, of course, is a difficult task. It is hard for a trade union to express an opinion, for example, on the price of meat. A pound of meat usually is too cheap for the one who is producing it, and too expensive for the one who is buying it. Therefore the trade union must have its internal organization structured in such a way that decision-makers can listen to all the different interests which, like everything else in our lives, are in constant confrontation.

After hearing all opinions in all the different organizations, the unions should give their judgment, based on arguments, to the people in the working organization. This requires internal reorganization in the trade unions. We need a teachers' trade union and a doctors' trade union; we need unions in all branches of the economy, to be able to function in such a way.

ADIZES: There is one basic reason why trade unions in Yugoslavia will further increase in power and importance. The original self-management system was based on the concept of unity of interests which is a principal component of communist ideology. With decentralization, conflicting interests began to surface and the unity of interests came under question. Who really represents the workers in a self-management system? Is it the Workers' Council? Or does it represent the total organization?

With decentralization, a multiplicity of interests emerged, and new institutional forms emerged to represent them. One of these is the Trade Union.

THE NORWEGIAN EXPERIENCE

THORSRUD: I will speak mainly from the Norwegian point of view; but most of what I am saying applies to Sweden and even more so to Denmark.

I do not think we get very far by defining democracy in terms of concepts. We can get further by clarifying the conditions under which democracy might arise. Incidentally, I think it much easier to define democracy in negative terms. To find a definition, you might ask those who are without it. (Sick people know what health is.)

There are three basic conditions for general democracy which have been described by political scientists such as Mannheim, but Mannheim made it quite clear that there are differences between formal and actual democracy.

The first of Mannheim's conditions is that people are equal as human beings. This means that people's humanity has to be taken for granted also in the work situation. Race, sex, etc., should not make them different. I do not think we in Norway should take it for granted that this condition is fulfilled in general, and certainly it is not fulfilled in industry; however, I do think other countries have more problems in this respect than we.

The second basic condition is freedom of participation. This means that if you want to participate you should be able to, without censorship or economic restrictions. This applies to general democracy, and even more so, to industrial democracy.

The third basic condition is that leadership is responsible to the many. This means that class, religion, or party, or any other type of closed elite does not have privileged access to and control over the leadership. And again, this applies not only to general democracy but to industrial democracy as well.

This was a fairly useful definition when the discussion of industrial democracy started to become more intense in Norway in 1960. In Sweden and Denmark it happened a little later, but today industrial democracy is one of the key political problems, and a major plank of the election platform of all political parties.

In 1961 we (I mean a group of people involved in a small applied research institute) were asked whether we were willing to work on this problem.

In Norway we are faced with two basic subjects: first, the formal aspect of representation, in terms of consultation or decision-making, etc., and, second, personal participation.

We took a hard look at companies where employees were represented on the Boards. That seemed to many people the most simple answer to the whole problem of industrial democracy. We did not think so. We intended to work mostly on personal participation.

The results of a one-year study of five companies where representation of employees on the board level had been practiced for a number of years are described in my attached article.

We agreed to work in the existing framework, in contrast to what happened in the Yugoslav situation. The reason for this is that Norwegian law is the codification of practiced social life. In some countries law is more an indication of the type of change that is desired; and there are many types of countries in between.

So we agreed to work within existing law, that is, within the terms of a very strong labor law through which you can solve almost any type of problem connected with your employment.

Second, we agreed to work within the existing bargaining structure, that is, the existence of very strong trade unions which in fifty years had established different basic conditions for industrial democracy, particularly on the formal level. We also accepted the fact that there existed strong associations of employees, and that there was a conciliation system through which government was strongly involved in the bargaining process.

Third, we agreed to work within the existing limits of productivity. This is a delicate point, because our efforts could have been interpreted as merely an attempt to improve productivity. This was not the case, but we could not overlook problems of productivity.

So this was the context within which we were to work, but of course we made it quite clear that, as social scientists, we could not accept these constraints unless it was taken for granted that the democratization in the work place would inevitably imply institutional change.

We could not ignore the fact that we had had a continual growth of about six percent in GNP per annum and this, not starting from a primitive level, was a very high rate. Second, diversification of manufacturing was progressing very rapidly. For instance, whereas we used to buy our mechanical goods from Sweden, we were about to have Sweden as our major purchaser of such goods (e.g., subdeliveries for Volvos and Saabs). Third, our whole economy was in a process of reconstruction inasmuch as our forests, fishing grounds, waterfalls, and mines were becoming scarce and had lost importance in economic terms. Fourth, there had already been an explosion in higher education which was just about to reach industry.

We were transcending the welfare state because we had already reached it to a very great extent. (Incidentally, rather than saying the basic condition for self-management is social ownership, I would say that it is a satisfactory level of social justice.)

But we realized that a traditional welfare state had not given all that we hoped it would give. Certainly it had not abolished the conditions for widespread alienation. Nor had it solved a number of other problems. But now we were moving from the welfare state into an educational and service community, into the postindustrial era.

Finally, we had already more or less a Nordic market and we seemed to be heading toward a European market. And we knew that we were at a very precarious point of balance, where we were actually suggesting fundamental institutional change in a situation where we could not afford to jeopardize political stability.

Political stability is a basic condition for investment, particularly in shipping in Norway; our national pride rests on it. It is basic for small things giving us status in the outside world (such as joining with other Scandinavian countries in peacekeeping in the Gaza Strip).

These are the basic facts of life that we want to live with. This does not mean that we want to consider ourselves a model of harmony. I do not think we can deal with change without having to cope with a great deal of stress and conflict.

As I said before, in comparison to Yugoslavia which went the revolutionary way, we have tended to pursue industrial democracy within given conditions and institutional arrangements prevalent in Norway. We pursued change in an evolutionary manner. The strategy the social scientists group undertook was as follows.

In the first place, we had to specify the criteria we wanted to use to evaluate the new system as against the old. For this purpose we gathered all the information available around 1960 regarding sociological and psychological research on dissatisfaction in work. We established six simple criteria of job and organizational design to indicate the direction in which we wanted the organization to move. We had to build into the man-machine or the man-task relationship an optimum level of variety. And I am talking now about the shop floor. Unless you increase participation on the shop floor, there will be need to supervise people in an old fashioned way. If that happens, then you need supervisors and middle management to supervise the supervisors in an old fashioned way, and you will have a top management that will focus its main attention on the inside instead of on the outside of the company, which should be its primary task. I do not mean that there has to be something new all the time in terms of variety, but there has to be enough to give meaning to work, enough so that you can change from a rapid spurt to a slower pace of work, etc.

Second, learning has to be part of the job, and not only once but as a continuous process. This means you cannot construct a job in such a way that you teach everybody a very narrow task with very little variation, but rather, you create jobs with variation and learning, which reinforce each other. If you have variation you have learning, and if you have learning you can utilize variation because you have better understanding of what you are doing.

Third, the decision-making capability must be increased, and you do that by starting to coordinate. A certain amount of decision-making must be built concretely into the job.

Fourth, you have to create conditions for social support within the organization so that people feel that they are necessary and respected.

Fifth, you have to relate the job to the outside world, which is very difficult under some conditions and much easier under some others.

And sixth, you must relate the job to the needs of the future.

But let me now pass to some more concrete examples of what we are actually doing. Let me indicate very briefly the type of steps we may take in a company. We engage in a study of the technology and the social system (these two are interacting). We choose a department which is strategically placed in the company, and we study the department and derive proposals from our own analysis as well as from the people there.

This is the first part of the experiment. Until this point, it is an experiment done by outsiders, which can be stopped and remain an experiment. But we have to conduct the experiment in such a way that it starts a growing process in the organization itself.

In our first field experiment it seemed to us that partly autonomous work groups would be most suitable to initiate a continuous organization of change. One of the concrete conditions we had to change was the role of the foreman. Second, we had to find forty-six men on five to seven benches, and let them handle their work as a group and not as individuals. We had to change the wage structure from individual piece rates to a bonus on what they produced as a group. Furthermore, we had to arrange job rotation to have greater flexibility.

We had to put a time limit on our study so that the company could be sure that they could get rid of us and of the experiment after evaluation. They had to be included in the evaluation, as part of the democratization process.

We looked at the company as part of an environment. We looked at the goals of the company as defined by the interrelations between the company and the raw materials; the company and the technological change outside; the company and capital (defined both in concrete and abstract terms); the company and the sales system; the company and the local institutions, such as the local trade school, etc.

In our second experiment we could create an action group to guide the development. We have interesting tapes from its discussions. The men started to talk about "our" theory. And in that group was a process worker, a foreman, and an assistant training manager. They talked about "our" model of the company, and "our" model of change, and "our" strategy of change.

There really was nothing entirely new introduced in the experiments that had not been there before. The main thing we did was to make things explicit so that they could be used as steppingstones to a road toward increased democracy.

After four experiments between 1961 and 1969, involving studies in personal participation in manufacturing industry, we were invited to go into the shipping industry and education.

If you experiment in a ship you really have to look into the future. Will there be anybody on board? Probably yes. If there are crews involved, how many people should we have in order to have a social system? What are we hiring sailors for? Can we hire better educated men and women? (Today there are a lot of women on board Norwegian ships, doing highly skilled jobs.) What will life be like on board ships? Will education be different from what it is now?

We cannot design an organization for a ship unless we look at these factors. This is one of the main reasons why we are now working in the field of education. Unless we work with education now, education will not be able to furnish to this type of organization the people we need, and we will have a terrible clash between work organizations and educational institutions.

In the organization of research and development there are four basic steps in changes. The first is information: if you do not share information you cannot even start a change process based on participation. But you do not share very much until you have started.

Second, there is a state of involvement, and it is only when you have involvement that you have a higher level of information. This, incidentally, is one of the reasons for the split at the bottom of a company to which I referred before. If people are not involved, they do not ask important questions, and they do not get and give important information.

The third stage is one of commitment. You have to commit yourself to a certain change so that you can evaluate what you have done when you accomplish your task.

Fourth, you may have *joint action.* You have to accept that this is a joint venture. Change is not something you can do alone. You are in fact doing research and development with a lot of people, and we can see within our own research and development organization that, in eight years, we have completely changed our old ideas of social research.

ROCK: For the last 150 years, the men you are working with, have been conditioned to work as cogs in a machine, and so I should think that when you approach a factory with these changes, you are confronted with people who are really bored and unhappy, and yet quite conservative. Thus, unless there is a change in consciousness, these structural changes cannot really take place. I wonder, since you are trying to impose structural changes, how do you deal with this problem?

THORSRUD: I cannot accept the word "impose." We are tendering a process of growth in terms of concrete conditions. But you are right. On the shop floor level, we often meet the type of people you indicated. And it is not that they might not be interested and able to participate. Rather, they have been for too long subject to the vicious circle of demotivation. This is why the experiment has to be tested. If it does not work on the shop floor level, it will not work at all. Even in countries like Norway or the United States, you still have 20 percent of the population in a job structure which is basically a slave structure in terms of the content of the jobs. And it is not easy to enhance their willingness to cooperate. There have been too many systems imposed on them, and this would seem to be just another one.

CONCLUSIONS

ANDERSON: I find that self-management, like education, remains an unending process. We can grasp elements of what it is, but it is impossible to comprehend it in its entirety.

We have discussed many of the questions pertinent to self-management. Among others, we explored the question of the conditions necessary for self-management to develop. I personally concluded that, first, one must not be dogmatic, but that environment, prevailing concepts, and leadership are important. In the best of circumstances, one should be looking for a combination of desires and motivation, social encouragement, and political acceptance, to provide a climate for the growth of self-management. Failure to have all of these elements in harmony does not necessarily mean that it is impossible to begin a process of self-management, but probably it forebodes a bleak future for its development, unless these elements are harmonized.

One of the questions with regard to the optimum mechanism for starting and growing self-managment is the following: does the Yugoslav experience tell us how to do the job in other countries? Do the Israeli kibbutz or the Norwegian experiments provide models for the developing countries or for the developed countries?

I personally conclude that these are wrong questions. They miss the point. It is vital to recognize that self-management is an ongoing process. If we take it out of context or assume that it must serve all needs in a universal fashion, we empty it of its substance. The best way to move may be to take advantage of the proper climate and a pragmatic willingness to analyze the concrete situation and to begin the effort, and then later to analyze and to change the effort.

We asked: is self-management an end in itself? The answer is no. Self-management is a part of the drive for self-development and the growth of personal freedom and responsibility. It is a means for achieving growth in people. That, in itself, means a continuing evolution of self-management, as individuals learn and grow in their developing society.

This process is an evolving one and basically we help it in the same way in which we help people to grow and evolve.

The best method, probably, for spreading and teaching the lessons of self-management is the case study method. In other words, no universal theory or solution can be applied to all situations. Each case must be analyzed within its own environment. From this I conclude that the serious study of self-management will include case studies.

Let me make a few recommendations for future research.

First, it seems to me that if I am correct with respect to my conclusion on the case study method, then we should more seriously try to develop an international body of case studies for study by serious students who hope to be involved in the propagation of self-management throughout the world. The compilation of such case studies, and the realization that any situation has to be matched with tools and techniques, could be an important contribution to the spread of self-management.

My second recommendation is inspired by our Yugoslav colleagues. When we speak of self-management, we tend to think of the material production part of society. I suspect that we could gain a lot if we deliberately reverse that emphasis and talk about some of the experiments and some of the conclusions that have been reached in self-management in the service sectors of society, and in the governmental sector of society. These sectors are so important in our life today; self-management in them may be the best cure for our bureaucratic ailments.

My third recommendation is somewhat more vague. It is that we should commit ourselves to a more thoughtful development of the tools for evaluation which have been found successful in the self-management experiments. The first questions to be asked are these: how do you know that it works? How do you measure that it is better than what you had before? How do you evaluate the benefits to the people involved in the experiment? If we could have better tools for evaluation and explanations of the educational process that occurs in self-management, this would be useful in convincing others of the need for self-management.

BORGESE: My first conclusion is that self-management obviously is a subject of profound importance, and this is attested to by the presence of participants from so many countries and walks of life, as well as by the unusually large audience we have here.

The second conclusion is that self-managment means many things to many people. It may be a public-relations stunt; it may be a means to get more out of the workers, to cut costs; it may be a mental-health medicine; it may be a research project, an experiment; and it may be a revolution.

Third, we have not really heard from any one here that self-management is not a good thing, or that it is a bad thing. We have heard from only one participant that although it is an excellent thing we cannot have it, that it has no place in our real world, and that it is utopian.

In other words, the arguments that we have heard against self-management are the same we have heard against world-management, world organization, world government. It is argued, that is, that first we need a new consciousness, a new community; and the obstacles on the road toward both self-management and world-management have been described in the same terms. They are the existing structure of property,

the existing structure of sovereignty, and the existing structure of hierarchy and power. Of course one could answer that consciousness and community may be learned "on the job" of building self-management and
building world-management. The obstacles that have been mentioned are
hollow, and how long they will be able to keep up their facade, no one can
tell.

Thus, the question as to the preconditions for the establishment of
self-management seems to me to be very difficult to answer; for what is
cause, and what is effect in the dialectics of history, who can tell. Self-
management and world-management are emerging from the ruins of the
present structures of property, sovereignty, hierarchy, and power; and
they are hastening the ruination of these structures. Those who are building self-management on this uncertain and shifting basis will be frustrated
and disappointed one thousand times. They will be criticized and attacked,
but that is the only way things move, and perfection is not of this world.
Those who leave the future to the future, practically defend the status
quo.

What are the means and the mechanisms to transform an enterprise
into a community?

Well, the first means, it seems to me, is the clarification of the goal. It
is the design of the structure. This, obviously, is where institutions like
ours can help and where thinking people from all countries can and must
cooperate. The second step depends on local and historical circumstances
and requires flexibility and adaptability. It may consist in starting from
scratch and rising from the ruins. It may be fighting. It may be taking to
the woods or the hills. It may be persuasion on the one hand, and
enlightened abdication on the other. I personally believe that it will be a
long, bitter, and in a way, a never ending struggle. Neither self-
management nor world-management are aims by themselves. They are
connected: they are the two poles of decentralization and integration between which men at this stage of history are regrouping as on a magnetic
field, with the old structures still sticking up and being dissolved slowly by
a process of electrolysis, you might say, but still standing there and dis-
torting the pattern. I think that a self-management system integrated in a
world-management system provides the best institutional and constitutional instrument for the long-range and multiple, or polyvalent,
liberation and development of human resources.

ADIZES: Self-management has a number of advantages over other sociopolitical and economic systems. First, it is by definition decentralized, and
in an increasingly complex environment, decentralization is one way to
survival.

Second, it facilitates change because by definition the system
discourages any power inherent in fixed roles. Capability to change is a
necessity in the turbulent environment facing us.

Third, by definition, self-management means actual capability of
members of systems to effectively participate. Thus, self-management
necessarily creates a learning environment, since an individual cannot effectively participate unless he knows what he is participating in. The

future poses increasing challenges for modern society to establish such learning environments if it wants to adapt promptly to new conditions.

Fourth, self-management by definition, precludes monopolization of power by any input and thus the distinction is eliminated between workers and management as two different groups with unequal prerogatives to decide for each other. This in itself has more than mere humanistic value. In an environment of ever increasing technological complexity, with increasing exploitation of the physical environment, the goals of an organization become of concern not only to an elite group but to all the rest of the members of society. With the revolution in information delivery capability and with the increased educational levels of blue collar workers, all groups in society have the capability to determine goals. The responsibility for survival becomes the task not only of an exclusive social group, but of all those that share the space in which they live.

Fifth, self-management enhances capital formation by encouraging higher levels of sacrifice today for higher levels of benefits tomorrow. This is inherent in the system since all participants make the decisions democratically and share in the results. Thus, it is assumed that no one's sacrifice today will yield rewards to someone else tomorrow. A system that enhances capital formation should be encouraged since it is a necessity for developing nations.

Sixth, self-management as a system bypasses one of the significant bottlenecks of developing nations. It encourages group entrepreneurship and management when both entrepreneurship and managerial know-how are scarce. Thus, self-management is an "ongoing school," generating the human resources that are scarce for developing nations.

The seventh reason that I support self-management is that the system encourages the search for objective truth. There is no adequate participation without full disclosure of information, and information monopolization leads to inequities in power distribution. Once information is open, full participation necessarily leads closer to truth than would monopolization of that information and its subsequent manipulation by any special group. The search for objective truth away from subjective truth based on inadequately resolved conflicts of interests is, in my opinion, what humanity is all about.

The eighth reason for supporting self-management is humanistic in nature. When we propose to eliminate the management-labor distinction (a necessary elimination if each participant is to have equal influence on decisions as claimed in the definition of self-management), we might restore in the human being involved, the sense of being more than just an input for production to be used for someone else's purpose.

The system in Yugoslavia is closest to developed self-management. It is still on the road to fully actualizing it, a claim with which Yugoslav theoreticians are the first to agree. However, different people see different barriers on this road. Some of these are particularly important. In my opinion, lack of recognition of capital contribution on an individual basis is one of those barriers. At present, capital formation encourages certain monopolistic or oligopolistic concentrations of capital, both of which might lead to a new form of self-managed capitalism or technocratism.

A mechanism for capital mobility without concentration of power should be established. Any fear that private ownership via a stock market will lead to monopolization of decision-making by the shareholders is not based on a real understanding of how companies are managed, for instance, in capitalist societies. Shareholder interests are more of a constraint upon management than the exclusive force behind corporate decision-making. Thus in self-management, capital can be used but it should be diffused among many shareholders, rather than having mutual funds or banks be the exclusive source of capital, in order to ensure that capital sources do not unite to impose their interest upon the company and seriously undermine the labor's control of the company's decision-making. Probably these individual shareholders will be mostly workers in the company, with shares (bonds) distributed in lieu of salary whenever the workers decide to reinvest some current revenues back into the company instead of distributing all the revenue as salary. The individual worker can retain some claim upon the future fruits of this sacrifice (via his bonds) without fear of losing these anticipated fruits if he moves to another company. In this way, the motivation to sacrifice for the future will be retained without discouraging labor mobility, and a multiple source of capital can be generated without having the banks or companies provide it. When banks or companies lend money, their power is not diffused, and they are definitely a powerful force which limits labor's discretion in decision-making.

All this is necessary if labor and capital mobility are to be achieved. Without those two, there is no adequate market mechanism. The more imperfect the market mechanism, the higher the inconsistency of rewards as related to contributions, which in turn means the worse is self-management.

A second significant barrier to self-management as practiced in Yugoslavia is that it denies the importance of the executive group. The more poorly trained this group is, the more faulty will be the process of decision-making and the greater will be the pressure to eliminate self-management and move to technocratia. Failing results and external pressures have throughout history turned democracy to anarchy or dictatorship. Yugoslavia needs to train a new breed of democratic community leaders for its organizations. The function of coordination, organization, planning and organizational structuring cannot be eliminated. A new theory of management, new executive attitudes, new tools of mobilization and motivation have to be created for adequate self-management.

In a democracy it is essential that every citizen is educated as a potential President. In a self-management system, likewise, every worker must be educated as a potential Chairman of the Board.

SELECTED BIBLIOGRAPHY

Books

Adizes, Ichak. *Industrial Democracy: Yugoslav Style.* New York: Free Press, 1971.

Bilandzic, Dusan. *Management of Yugoslav Economy, 1945-1966.* Beograd: Yugoslav Trade Unions, 1967.

———. *Social Self-Government.* Beograd: 1965, No. 1, "Medjunardona Politika."

Blumberg, P. *Industrial Democracy: The Sociology of Participation.* New York: Schocken Books, 1969.

Broekmeyer, M.J. *Yugoslav Workers' Self Management.* Dordrecht, Holland: D.Reidel Publishing Company.

Clegg, H. A. *A New Approach to Industrial Democracy.* Oxford: 1963.

Confederation of Trade Unions in Yugoslavia. *How Do the Working Collectives Distribute Creative Values.* Beograd: 1964.

Derber, Milton. *The American Idea of Industrial Democracy.* Chicago: University of Illinois Press, 1970.

Horvat, B. *An Essay on the Yugoslav Society.* White Plains, New York: International Arts and Sciences Press, 1969.

———. *Towards a Theory of Planned Economy.* Beograd: Yugoslav Institute of Economic Research, 1964.

International Labor Office. *Workers' Management in Yugoslavia.* Geneva: 1962.

International Labor Office. *Participation of Workers in Decisions Within Undertakings.* Geneva: International Labor Office, 1969.

Kolaja, J. *A Polish Factory, A Case Study of Workers' Participation in Decision-Making.* Lexington: University of Kentucky Press, 1960.

Kolaja, Jiri. *Workers' Councils: The Yugoslav Experiences.* New York: F.A. Prager, 1966, p. 84.

Milenkovitch, Deborah D. *Plan and Market in Yugoslav Economic Thought.* New Haven: Yale University Press, 1971.

Pejovic, S. *The Market Planned Economy of Yugoslavia.* Minneapolis: University of Minnesota Press, 1966.

Singleton, F., and Topham, A. *Workers Control in Yugoslavia.* London: Fabian Society, 1963.

Sturmthal, A. *Workers' Councils.* Cambridge, Massachusetts: Harvard University Press, 1964.

153

———. *Workers' Councils—A Study of Workplace Organization on Both Sides of the Iron Curtain.* Cambridge, Massachusetts: Harvard University Press, 1964.

Thorsrud, E. and Emery, F.E. *Form and Content in Industrial Democracy.* London: Tavistock, 1970.

Vanek, Jam. *The Economics of Workers' Management.* London: George Allen and Unwin Ltd., 1972.

Vanek, Jaroslav. *General Theory of Labor Managed Market Economies.* Ithaca, New York: Cornell University Press, 1971.

———. *The Participatory Economy.* Ithaca, New York: Cornell University Press, 1971.

Vucinich, W. S., ed. *Contemporary Yugoslavia: Twenty Years of Socialist Experiment.* Berkeley, California: University of California Press, 1969.

Ward, B. *The Socialist Economy.* New York: Random House, 1967.

Waterston, Albert. *Planning in Yugoslavia.* Washington, D.C.: Economic Development Institute, 1962.

Articles

Adizes, I. "Economic Changes in Yugoslavia." *East Europe* 21:10 (October 1972).

———. "The Role of Management in Democratic (Communal) Organizational Structures." *Annals of Public and Cooperative Economy* 4(1971), pp. 399-420.

———, and F. Weston. "Comparative Models of Social Responsibilily." *Journal of the Academy of Management* 2:1 (March 1973).

Bajt, A. "Decentralized Decision-Making Structure in the Yugoslav Economy." *Economics of Planning* 7:1 (1967), pp. 73-85. Oslo.

———. "Yugoslav Economic Reforms, Monetary and Production Mechanism." *Economics of Planning* 7:3 (1967).

Bicanic, R. "Economic Growth Under Centralized and Decentralized Planning, Yugoslavia—A Case Study." In *Comparative Economic Systems, A Reader,* pp. 271-287. New York: Random House, 1969.

Burk, G. "Socialist Enterprise That Acts Like a Fierce Capitalist Competitor." *Fortune,* January 1972.

Cox, Robert et al. "Workers' Participation in Management." *International Institute for Labour Studies Bulletin,* February 1967, pp. 65-125.

Demsetz. H. "Towards a Theory of Property Rights." *American Economic Review,* May 1965, pp. 247-59.

Dubravcic, D. "Labor as Entrepreneurial Input: An Essay in the Theory of the Producer Co-operative Economy." *Economica,* August 1970.

Fisher, J.C. "City Planning and Housing Administration in Yugoslavia." *Urban Affairs Quarterly,* December 1965, pp. 1-13.

———. "The Yugoslav Commune." *World Politics,* no. 3 (April 1964), pp. 418-41.

Furubotn, E. "Towards a Dynamic Model of the Yugoslav Firm." *Canadian Journal of Economics,* May 1971.

Furubotn, and S. Pejovich. "The Role of the Banking System in Yugoslav Economic Planning, 1946-1969." *Revue Internationale d'Histoire de la Banque* 4(Summer 1971), pp. 51-91. Geneve.

Gorupic, D. "Trends in the Development of Workers' Self-Management in Yugoslavia." *Eastern European Economics* 8:2(1969-70), pp. 101-182. New York.

Gorupic, D. and I. Paj. *Workers' Self-Management in Yugoslav Undertakings.* Ekonomski institut Zagreb, 1970. Zagreb.

Horvat, B. "Planning and the Market: The Yugoslav Experience." *Planning and Development Programming, O.E.C.D.* 1964. Paris.

———. "Yugoslav Economic Policy in the Post-War Period." *American Economic Review* 61:3 (June 1971).

Jerovsek, J. "Self-Management in Working Organizations from the Point of View of Efficiency and Democracy." *U.N. Conference,* October 1969. Herceg Novi.

———. "The Structure of Influence in the Yugoslav Commune." *Atlantis* 2(1970), pp. 31-48.

Kavcic, B., V. Rus, and A. S. Tannenbaum. "Control, Participation and Effectiveness in Four Yugoslav Organizations." *Administrative Science Quarterly,* March 1971.

Kolaja, J. "A Yugoslav Workers' Council." *Human Organization* 1(1961), pp. 27-31.

Kostic, C. "Peasant Industrial Workers in Yugoslavia." *Man in India* 39 (1959), pp. 221-34.

Kukoleca, S. "Review of Movements in Yugoslav Economy Toward Decentralization." *Economic Hearings 8th Congress,* 2nd Session Part 7a, 4495-4506.

Leenian, W. A. "Syndicalism in Yugoslavia." *Economic Development and Cultural Change* 18:2 (January 1970), pp. 230-39.

Loucks, W. "Workers' Self-government in Yugoslav Industry." *World Politics,* October 1958, pp. 68-82.

Lukic, R. "Self-Management and Consumers." *Review of International Affairs,* nos. 408-409 (Beograd, 1967), pp. 21, 16.

Markovic, M. "Employment Relationships Under the Yugoslav System of Management of the Workers." *International Labour Review* 79:2 (1959), pp. 141-57.

Marschak, T. "Centralized Versus Decentralized Resource Allocation; The Yugoslav Laboratory." *Quarterly Journal of Economics,* November 1968, pp. 561-87.

Mladek, J. V., et al. "The Change in the Yugoslav Economic System." *International Monetary Fund Staff Papers* 3:3 (November 1952), pp. 407-38.

Montias, John Michael. "Economic Reform and Retreat in Yugoslavia." *Foreign Affairs* 37:2 (January 1959), pp. 293-305.

Neal, Fred Warner. "The Communist Party in Yugoslavia." *American Political Science Review* 51:1 (March 1957), pp. 88-111.

————. "The Reforms in Yugoslavia." *American Slavic and East European Review* 13(April 1954), pp. 227-44.

————. "Yugoslav Communist Theory." *American Slavic and East European Review* 19:1 (1960), pp. 42-62.

Neal, F. W. and Fisk. "Yugoslavia: Towards a Market Socialism." *Problems of Communism,* November-December 1966, pp. 28-37.

Neuberger, E. "The Yugoslav Investment Auctions." *Quarterly Journal of Economics* 72:1 (1959), pp. 88-115.

Neuberger, E. and E. James "The Yugoslav Self-Managed Enterprise: A Systemic Approach." In *Plan and Market,* edited by M. Bornstein. New Haven and London: Yale Universiy Press, 1973.

Obradovic, S. "Employment Trends and Problems in Yugoslavia." *International Labour Review* 95:6 (1967), pp. 55-71. Geneva.

————. "Participation and Work Attitudes in Yugoslavia." *Industrial Relations Journal* (Berkeley), February 1970, pp. 161-69.

Obradovic, S., J. French, and L. Rodgers. "Workers Councils in Yugoslavia: Effects on Perceived Participation and Satisfaction of Workers." *Human Relations* 23:5 (October 1970).

Popov. "The Problem of Strikes in Yugoslavia." Reprinted in *International* 1:7 (January-February 1972).

Pusic, E. "The Interdependence between Social and Economic Planning with Special Reference to Yugoslavia." In *Social Welfare Policy,* edited by Ponsioen, pp. 239-87. The Hague: Mouton and Co., 1962.

Rawin, S.J. "Social Values and the Managerial Structure—The Case of Yugoslavia and Poland." *Journal of Comparative Administration,* August 1970.

Ridell, David S. "Social Self-government: The Background of Theory and Practice in Yugoslav Socialism." *British Journal of Sociology,* March 1968.

Rockwell, C.S. "An International Comparison of the Size and Efficiency of the Yugoslav Plant." Center Discussion Paper Number 47, Economic Growth Center, Yale University, February 1968.

————. "The Relevance of Illyria for Less Developed Countries." Center Discussion Paper Number 56, Economic Growth Center, Yale University, June 1968.

Rus, V.. "Influence Structure in Yugoslav Enterprises." *Industrial Relations Journal* (Berkeley), February 1970.

Sacks, S. R. "Changes in Industrial Structure in Yugoslavia. 1959-1968." *Journal of Political Economy* 80:3 (May-June 1972).

Samardzija, M. and G. Klein. "Perspective View of Self-Management in a Socialist Context." 66th Meeting of the American Political Science Association, Los Angeles, September 1970.

Sefer, B. "Income Distribution in Yugoslavia." *International Labour Review* 97:4 (1968), pp. 371-90.

Sen, A K. "Labor Allocation in a Cooperative Enterprise." *Review of Economic Studies,* October 1966, pp. 316-71.

Singleton, F. "Yugoslav Self-Management." *New Left Review* 18(1963), pp. 73-84.

Solomon, J. "Social Values and the Managerial Structure: The Case of Yugoslavia and Poland." *Journal of Comparative Administration,* August 1970, pp. 131-59.

Stanovnik, J. "Planning Through the Market." *Foreign Affairs* 40:2 (January 1960), pp. 252-63.

Strauss, G. and E. Rosenstein. "Workers' Participation: A Critical View." *Industrial Relations Journal* (Berkeley), February 1970.

Sukijasovic, M. "The Yugoslav System of Self-management and Joint Business Ventures with Foreign Private Firms; Legal Aspects." *Review of International Affairs* nos. 416-417 (Beograd, 1967), pp. 29-32.

Supek, R. "Some Contradictions and Insufficiencies of Yugoslav Self-Managing Socialism." *Praxis* (International Edition) 8:3-4 (1971).

Sweezy, Paul. "The Yugoslav Experiment." *Monthly Review* 9:11 (1958), pp. 362-73.

Tanic, Zivan. "Social Composition of Workers' Councils in Yugoslavia." *Indian Journal of Industrial Relations* 3:1 (July 1967), pp. 19-40.

UNESCO. "The Yugoslav Commune." *International Social Science Journal* 13:3 (1961), pp. 379-448.

Vanek, J. "Decentralization under Workers' Management: A Theoretical Appraisal." *American Economic Review,* December 1969.

Vratusa, A. "Yugoslav Commune." *UNESCO* 23:3 (1961), pp. 379-448.

Wachtel, Howard M. "Workers' Management and Interindustry Wage Differentials in Yugoslavia." *Journal of Political Economy* 80:3 (May-June 1972).

Ward, Benjamin. "The Firm in Illyria: Market Syndicalism." *American Economic Review,* September 1958.

———. "Industrial Decentralization in Yugoslavia." *California Slavic Studies* 2(1963), pp. 169-187.

———. "Marxism-Horvatism: A Yugoslav Theory of Socialism." *American Economic Review,* June 1967, pp. 509-23.

———."Political Power and Economic Change in Yugoslavia." *American Economic Review,* Papers and Proceedings, May 1968, pp. 568-79.

———. "Workers' Management in Yugoslavia." *Journal of Political Economy,* 1957, pp. 373-86.

Zaninovich, M. G. "Elites and Citizenry in Yugoslav Society: A Study of Value Differentiation." In *Comparative Communist Political Leadership.* New York: David McKay Co., 1973.

Zupanov, J. "The Producer and Risk." *Eastern European Economies,* Spring 1969, pp. 12-28.

Zupanov, J. and A. S. Tannenbaum. "Distribution of Influence in Some Yugoslav Industrial Organizations as Perceived by Members." In *Control in Organizations,* edited by A.S. Tannenbaum, pp. 91-109. New York: McGraw-Hill, 1968.

INDEX